T0269791

CHEF TEE'S
CARIBBEAN
KITCHEN

CHEF TEE'S CARIBBEAN KITCHEN

PHOTOGRAPHY BY CLARE WINFIELD

rps

RYLAND PETERS & SMALL
LONDON • NEW YORK

Designer Megan Smith
Editor Abi Waters
Head of Production Patricia Harrington
Creative Director Leslie Harrington
Editorial Director Julia Charles

Food Stylist Rosie Reynolds
Prop Stylist Max Robinson
Indexer Vanessa Bird

First published in 2023 by
Ryland Peters & Small
20–21 Jockey's Fields
London WC1R 4BW
and Ryland Peters & Small, Inc.
341 East 116th Street
New York NY 10029

www.rylandpeters.com

Text © Chef Tee 2023
Design and commissioned
photographs © Ryland Peters
& Small 2023

ISBN: 978-1-78879-510-4

10 9 8 7 6 5 4 3 2 1

The authors' moral rights have
been asserted. All rights reserved.
No part of this publication may be
reproduced, stored in a retrieval
system or transmitted in any
form or by any means electronic,
mechanical, photocopying or
otherwise, without the prior
permission of the publisher.

Printed and bound in China

CIP data from the Library of
Congress has been applied for.
A CIP record for this book is
available from the British Library.

NOTES

* Both British (metric) and
American (imperial plus US
cups) are included; however,
ts important not to alternate
between the two within a recipe.
* All spoon measurements are
level unless specified otherwise.
* All eggs are medium (UK) or
large (US), unless specified as
large, in which case US extra
large should be used. Uncooked
or partially cooked eggs should
not be served to the very old, frail,
young children, pregnant women
or those with compromised
immune systems.
* Ovens should be preheated
to the specified temperatures.
If using a fan-assisted oven,
adjust according to the
manufacturer's instructions.
* When a recipe calls for the
grated zest of citrus fruit, buy
unwaxed fruit and wash well
before using. If you can only
find treated fruit, scrub well in
warm soapy water before using.
* Rinsing raw meat or fish/
seafood in a solution made
with water and white vinegar
is considered key in Caribbean
culture, however this step is
entirely optional and depends
on the produce you have.

DISCLAIMER

The views expressed in this book
are those of the author but they
are general views only. Ryland
Peters & Small hereby exclude all
liability to the extent permitted
by law for any errors or omissions
in this book and for any loss,
damage or expense (whether
direct or indirect) suffered by
a third party relying on any
information in this book.

MIX
Paper from
responsible sources
FSC® C106563

CONTENTS

MY STORY

I've spent days trying to write the perfect introduction but the sincere truth is, I can't! So instead, let me be honest and tell you 'why' I cook and 'what' it does for me, which I'm sure will be something that we can all relate to.

Standing on a stool by my late mother's hip, cooking tuna and pasta, is perhaps the first thing I truly remember cooking and eating. I know, it might not be the most Caribbean dish you'd think of, but I promise you, we made it 'Caribbean' with the lashings of Encona hot pepper sauce that came later. Yes, you know the one, made with Jamaican Scotch bonnet peppers! Cooking that dish, and eating with her, is perhaps the happiest memory in my life… I chuckle, feeling warm and happy just remembering. The joyful smile spread across my face and feeling of safety never fails to return when I remember that autumnal dish. And that, there, is exactly why I cook.

For me, every cake I make reminds me of baking with my aunty 'P' in Streatham – making the trip to the shops on the weekends and paying 99p for the boxed baking kit of 'Greens' cupcakes, pure heaven! Every batch of marinade I produce reminds me of when I got my first food processor at the age of 17, and well… I just thought that I was Battersea's 'hottest chef around'! Even every batch of curried goat that I cook reminds me of the eureka moment when I managed to cook it on a large scale for the first time. Within 30 seconds, I was speed-dialling all my friends to tell them the good news. You see, cooking food reminds me of key moments and nostalgic traditions in my life. But I guess, most importantly, it simply reminds me of the people who I have loved most in my life. Cooking makes me happy.

People automatically presume I am a natural chef. The truth is I am far from it! I am a 'creative' more than a chef. I have dabbled in many industries: I love to sew, to play piano, to knit, to paint, to teach and to bake. And each skill has had its turn at shaping my life, but for now it seems that cooking has won. Although, don't be surprised to find me knitting from time to time! So, 'a Jack of all trades' you might think… well, actually not so much. Being lucky enough to have this platform means I can share openly that I suffer from forms of anxiety and depression. In fact, funnily enough, I don't even have the healthiest relationship with food. But when I express myself through any of my creative abilities or better yet, when I cook, my mind shakes off the worries of the world and gives me peace. Cooking is a creative form of meditation for me. I forget about the bills troubling me, I forget about deadlines stressing me, the weight of the world on my shoulders. I am in a realm where negativity can't penetrate the protective bubble of happiness that I have created. Instead of worrying, I am creating new memories and exploring the world I live in. I am expressing myself creatively. And that is why I cook.

Caribbean cuisine is a niche field of cooking but not necessarily a hard one to master. It does vary slightly from island to island and from household to household, but one of the key essences of cooking the Caribbean way is to simply enjoy it! Listen to music as you cook, judge a measurement a little bit with your eye perhaps, and just make the recipe your own. For example, the recipe calls for dried chilli flakes/hot pepper flakes but you might only have fresh chillies/chilis – so adapt and make do. Right there, that's what it's about! The big key to Caribbean food and creating those happy memories is often the informality. This is as well as developing recipes from our mistakes or improvizations. Also, to have a few key signature ingredients to hand – pimento berries, turmeric, allspice, rum and sugar cane are the distinctive flavours of the Caribbean, so must be included. With these elements you can't go wrong. I can't stress enough, there is no right or wrong way, but there is, most importantly, a style.

Many think cooking professionally or, indeed, cooking Caribbean food is hard, but the unvarnished truth is, you just need the heart of a keen home cook. When I began teaching myself how to cook, I avoided learning how to make fancy foams, crusts or using water baths because I don't recall any of that when I was younger. During my childhood, food was just about tasting good flavours and giving that comforting warm feeling inside. So, as a result, you will find simplicity in my recipes and in the methods used, as I find that this yields the best results. This book aims to teach and inspire anybody of any heritage to be able to cook the classic staples of Caribbean food in an unfussy and easy way.

A lot has happened in the past 2 years and it's gone by so quickly! Every positive has been a positive and every negative has turned into a positive lesson. I have grown as a person along the way, and as a chef. I will finish by saying that I have always called my journey a 'story', and I am so grateful to be able to share this chapter with you.

MY RESTAURANT JOURNEY

I guess the light-bulb moment happened when I was about 18 and working in a restaurant in Brixton. I was working on the bar, and I suddenly realized that three plantain could be bought for just £1 in Brixton Market, but then this could be more than tripled when sold in local restaurants. It dawned on me that 'there are hardly any Caribbean restaurants in London'. I knew there and then, that I wanted one...

I began soaking up the knowledge of every restaurant I worked in, and started teaching myself recipes for the restaurant I would open one day. One restaurant wouldn't teach me everything, so I moved on to other restaurants, and from each restaurant, I would take a little nugget of knowledge. In one establishment, I would learn about bookings, while another would teach me about wine. Eventually, after some hard graft, I was 20 and in a Michelin-starred restaurant possessed with the skills of a chef, sommelier, bookkeeper and receptionist and I was ready. But how would I get the money for a restaurant?

At this point, everyone who knew me knew that 'Viexfort' (Paradise Cove's original name) was my dream, but no one was prepared for what happened next. One busy summer breakfast shift, as I cleared one of my customer's plates who happened to run a government-backed business funding scheme, I began to tell her my dream and she gave me her details to apply for the funding. It wasn't enough for a restaurant, but if I could just prove that I could make a pop-up restaurant work, then I could crowd-fund for the rest. I quit my job, ploughing all my energy into my dream, vowing that 'the next restaurant I worked in would be my own'. I wrote an 80-page business plan and applied, and within just 2 weeks, I received a business loan to give it a go.

Being creative, I converted the front room of my flat into a massive, commercial kitchen! I signed up to several food delivery partners and, by August 2014, I was running my business from home. Suddenly, I had a real taste of running a food business. I had 10 members of staff, including care leavers – it was important to me to give care leavers this opportunity because of my time spent in care as a child. I ended up closing after just 5 months, but I knew my story wasn't finished. If I could make it work from home, then surely I could anywhere!

By chance, I told my story to one of my regular customers who happened to be a business investor. After closing down, I bravely reached out to him and convinced him to invest in me, in my story, and he believed I could do it as he knew my food was good. With a new budget of £50K, we searched high and low and attempted to secure a location for Paradise Cove, but were unsuccessful each time... so I gave up. I paused my dream. I became a primary school teacher instead, turning my skill of helping, into nurturing children.

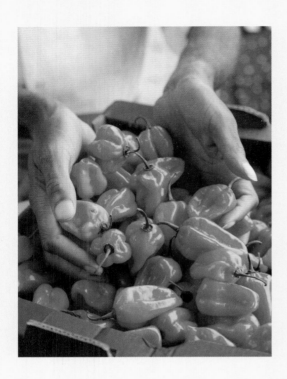

By the time the pandemic hit several years later, I had become deeply depressed. And made the life-changing decision to quit my career. I had four degrees, but I just felt like a failure. It was June 2020, I was 26 and I decided I was going to follow my dream and reopen again from my home, just like before. So on 1st July, I made the website, re-designed flyers, set up my social media… I was going to crowd-fund. I was excited and every day my mind zoomed with new ideas. To help manage this, I would go for a mindfulness walk every day. I was supposed to be meditating but actually, I was secretly visualizing where my restaurant would be. Then somehow, there it was… 517 Wandsworth road, with a sign, as clear as day, saying 'shop lease for sale!' Without hesitation, I called my friend Michael begging for his help. We spoke at length and he agreed to loan me some money, not enough but I could make it work. And with some clever negotiations, I got the keys to the shop the following evening on 19th July.

That same day, I ran to the nearest hardware store to pick up paints and began painting my restaurant. I searched online for all the secondhand cooking equipment I could find. I made my signs by hand, put up a new ceiling and used every creative trick I could to bring my restaurant to life. I was going for it with all that I had. It was single-handedly painted, floored and decorated by me. But I also contacted all my old suppliers from 6 years ago, and by some miracle, they all remembered me. 'You're the guy who cooked from home,' they would all say and all agreed to help me start with a small life-line of credit. Apart from the plumbing and electricity, I did it all alone. Somehow, I was ready to open on 5th August. My overdraft was overdrawn and I had nothing to my name. No money to pay my staff. No reputation. Nothing but determination and my dream.

Lickle Goals
- Be happy (By loving & accepting myself)
- Grow Mi 'family'
- Remain Humble (But allow myself to be proud...is ok!)
- Cook with mi heart
- Trust the greater Plan!
Chef Teé

The beginning was sensational. Locals flying in and the tail-end of summer caused an influx of customers and somehow, week after week, I never ran at a loss. Sometimes I had to sleep in the restaurant to make it work, but we slowly got busier and busier and made it work. Sadly the pandemic struck and we were forced to close, relying on takeaways to keep us going. Weirdly enough, I felt like I had done this bit before.

Seeing how well we were doing gave me ambition to expand. I hadn't even been at it 6 months and I wanted another restaurant. I found another shop and went for it. Slowly throughout the lockdowns, I ran one restaurant while preparing another for opening.

Fast-forward a year, we were still facing lockdowns and the second branch of the restaurant had closed. In hindsight, I had stretched myself too thin. I became unwell frequently. One of my landlords had passed away during the pandemic and the final blow was when someone decided to break into my restaurant and smash it to pieces. I gave up. I just couldn't cope with the repeated setbacks. But then, almost as if an act from God, 'it' happened... my community stepped in to save my restaurant. They raised over £10k to help it get new shutters, created a massive publicity campaign enabling us to feature on national TV, all resulting in a restaurant review by one of the country's most revered food critics, Jay Rayner. I was offered a TV show and a deal to write my own cookbook. Everyone believed in me and saw my ethical lickle restaurant striving to help the community. Within a very intense 2 weeks, we were saved... but I think I'll save the rest of that story for my next cookbook...

'Tropical blessings always, Tee'

MARINADES, RUBS & SAUCES

THE BASE OF ALL CARIBBEAN FOOD

When thinking of Caribbean food, it really is just too easy for us to 'only' consider the main dish. But the more I cook, the more I notice that most of our flavours actually come from the sauces and marinades that we start with first. You see, believe it or not, these versatile marinades are the key bases to all good Caribbean food – they create the depths of flavour that so many of us love. So, with that in mind, it is really important to get the balance of seasoning right, as the skill of building a 'good base' creates the perfect Caribbean meal.

Within the Black British community, Caribbean food can typically be associated with heavy pre-made dry seasonings. Since I started cooking, I have always found that using fresh, organic vegetables and better quality products really does yield the best results. I have also grown to make my recipes accessible to those with allergies and intolerances. So, in this section I have included a range of simple marinades, rubs and sauces, which reflect the best of that.

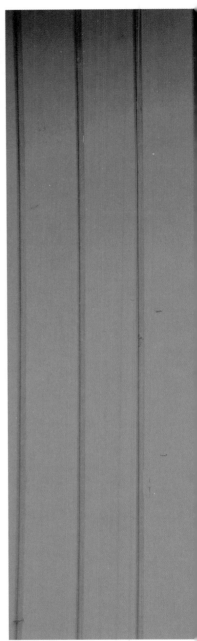

Above left: A fruit stall on the roads of the Dominican Republic. Above right: A tropical blue wall with bright pink window on a typical West Indian shack.

CHEF TEE'S SIMPLE JERK MARINADE

For those who don't know, jerk is a wet or dry marinade used to season dishes. Traditionally, it has been used for the flavouring and preserving of meats such as chicken and pork, as well as fish. However, it has now evolved with the new-age Caribbean cuisine movement and allowed for an array of plant-based jerk delicacies to be included, too. Jerk is synonymous with the Caribbean islands, but the real secret that makes jerk so distinctively unique is the use of pimento wood, or the now more commonly used, pimento berries. This is what gives jerk its special taste. Here is my take on this recipe for you to make your own.

1 lime, cut into quarters
15 g/½ oz. fresh thyme
100 g/3½ oz. Scotch bonnet pepper
150 g/5 oz. onion, topped and tailed
125 g/4½ oz. spring onions/scallions,
    topped and tailed
40 g/1½ oz. garlic cloves, peeled,
    topped and tailed
30 g/1 oz. pimento berries
15 g/½ oz. black peppercorns
2 tablespoons table salt
60 g/2 oz. granulated sugar
10 g/⅓ oz. ground cinnamon
5 g/1 teaspoon cloves
10 ml/2 teaspoons soy sauce
10 ml/2 teaspoons brown malt
    vinegar

MAKES ABOUT 500 G/1 LB. 2 OZ.

Place all the ingredients in a food processor or blender and pulse together to a smooth consistency.

Store in an airtight container in a cool, dry place for up to 6 months.

NOTE *If the blade sticks while you are blending, try adding water, a tablespoon at a time, and pulse until mixed.*

CHEF TEE'S JERK MARINADE PARTY MIX

Now you have mastered the classic jerk marinade (see opposite), I am sure you will want to host your own Caribbean barbecue (grill) party, so try this upscaled version instead. The method is slightly different but important to master for any chef wanting to turn their hand to cooking for a larger crowd.

90 g/3 oz. fresh thyme
80 g/3 oz. pimento berries
40 g/1½ oz. cloves
40 g/1½ oz. black peppercorns
450–600 g/16–21 oz. Scotch bonnet
   peppers, to taste
3.6 kg/8 lb. red and white onions,
   topped, tailed and quartered
100 g/3½ oz. spring onions/
   scallions, topped and tailed
350 g/12½ oz. garlic cloves (this is
   roughly 7–8 bulbs of garlic), peeled
5 large lemons, quartered
80 g/3 oz. table salt
600 g/3 cups granulated sugar
80 ml/⅓ cup soy sauce
80 ml/⅓ cup brown malt vinegar
60 g/2 oz. ground cinnamon

*A clean bucket or very large
   container with a lid*

MAKES ABOUT 5 LITRES/1.3 GALLONS

Chop the thyme sprigs in half, then pulse in a food processor or blender until finely blended. The processor will get hot when doing this from the moisture and friction, so make sure you hold onto it carefully. Transfer to a clean bucket or very large container when done.

Blend the pimento berries and cloves in the food processor or blender until semi-crushed, then add to the bucket.

Blitz the peppercorns in the food processor or blender until semi-crushed, then add to the bucket.

Add the Scotch bonnet peppers to the food processor and blitz until semi-crushed, then add to the bucket.

Blitz the onions and spring onions in the food processor until mashed, then add to the bucket when done.

Blitz the garlic cloves in the food processor until mashed, then add to the bucket.

Blitz the lemons in the food processor until mashed, then add to he other ingredients in the bucket.

Finally, add the salt, sugar, soy sauce, vinegar and cinnamon to the bucket. Mix everything together until blended into one delicious marinade.

Store in an airtight container in a cool, dry place for up to 6 months.

NOTES
★ *Check for any unblended lumps of ingredients as you transfer each one to the bucket and re-blend in smaller batches if necessary.*

★ *This recipe creates enough marinade for large parties or barbecues – it would roughly marinade enough meat for around 50 people, so save it for when you are entertaining a crowd!*

SIMPLE OXTAIL OR LAMB RUB

Before I start, it is important to acknowledge that a large proportion of the Caribbean's 'documented' history was interrupted by the transatlantic slave trade. The impact of this means that the cooking we now know as distinctly Caribbean is actually a blend of many other cultures. Our famous dishes and ingredients are really bits of Portuguese, African and Indian heritage to say the least. But they all commonly include the theme of working with cheaper cuts of meat, which often need long braising. This explains why some of our delicious delicacies are often snubbed and why I didn't actually eat them until I was in my late teens! It's no secret that oxtail falls under this remit, but when it is done right, it's simply sensational.

As it is often a fatty cut of meat, I would suggest following the instructions on page 113 if you want to use this rub with oxtail. However, the rub also works wonders on any more commonly used red meat, so feel free to pair it with your favourite lamb or beef recipe accordingly.

1 bulb of garlic, cloves
   separated and peeled
1 large onion, chopped
5 g/¼ oz. fresh thyme
thumb-sized piece of fresh ginger
1 Scotch bonnet pepper
1 teaspoon pimento berries
3 tablespoons good-quality
   vegetable bouillon or stock
   powder (I use Marigold vegetable
   stock powder)
1 teaspoon freshly ground black
   pepper
60 ml/¼ cup dark soy sauce

**MAKES ENOUGH TO MARINADE
1 KG/2¼ LB. OXTAIL**

Put the garlic cloves and onion into a food processor and pulse until fully blended. Add the thyme, ginger and Scotch bonnet pepper and pulse again until fully blended. Add the pimento berries, bouillon and black pepper and pulse again. Finally, pour in the soy sauce and pulse once more until fully combined.

Transfer to an airtight container and store in the fridge for up to 1 week, unless using right away.

To use with oxtail, follow the instructions on page 113.

SIMPLE ALL-PURPOSE PLANT-BASED MARINADE

Although jerk is a great marinade, slightly different seasonings are required when cooking more delicate dishes. This simple all-purpose marinade keeps the essence of Caribbean flavours. With less heat it is great for plant-based dishes, but in our busy working world it's also a quick way to add flavour to any dish. Rather than using salt and pepper to season, simply try seasoning with a couple of teaspoons of this instead before frying or roasting your chosen dish. Add it to rice, pasta, sauces or even dips... the possibilities are endless.

30 g/1 oz. fresh thyme
10 g/⅓ oz. pimento berries
10 g/⅓ oz. crushed black
    peppercorns
150 g/3½ oz. white onion,
    topped, tailed and quartered
100 g/3½ oz. red onion,
    topped, tailed and quartered
1 bulb of garlic, cloves separated
    and peeled
3 lemons, quartered
2 limes, quartered
35 g/1¼ oz. table salt
150–200 g/¾–1 cup granulated sugar
30 ml/2 tablespoons soy sauce
30 ml/2 tablespoons white wine
    vinegar

MAKES ABOUT 500 G/1 LB. 2 OZ.

Place all the ingredients in a food processor or blender and pulse together to a smooth consistency. Transfer to an airtight container and store in the fridge for up to 14 days, unless using right away.

SERVING SUGGESTION
Preheat the oven to 200°C fan/220°C/420°F/gas 7. Roughly chop up a selection of your favourite vegetables – red (bell) peppers, mushrooms, courgettes/zucchini and red onions work well. Add to a large roasting tin with 2 tablespoons water, rub in 3 tablespoons of the marinade and drizzle with a little oil of your choice. Cover the tray with foil and roast in the preheated oven for about 20–30 minutes until the vegetables have steamed. Remove the foil, then continue for another 20 minutes until the vegetables have caramelized.

For another serving suggestion, see Martinique-style Veg on page 79.

JAMAICAN SCOTCH BONNET HOT SAUCE

I was one of many growing up Black in London in the 1990s, but no matter the house, there were just some unspoken Caribbean rules that had to be followed. A rainbow fish in every front room (that you were never allowed to go into as it was only for visitors), silly doilies everywhere that really served no purpose, wooden carvings and Jamaican poems on the wall… I mean the list goes on really. But I learned at a young age that the ultimate unspoken rule, which my mum taught me, was undoubtedly that there must always be hot pepper sauce in the house!

Now, my mum, being a second-generation Black British woman, would buy her pepper sauce from the world food section in our local supermarket. But both my nans – one Jamaican and one St Lucian – would always make theirs from scratch. To this day, I can still vividly recall the recycled jars with pickled peppers, perching ever so inquisitively upon their kitchen fridges. This lickle recipe is a nod to both their recipes.

NOTES

★ *It is important to keep whisking this mix as the sugars can catch on the bottom of the pan. If this happens, soak the pan overnight and use a scourer in the morning to remove any crust left on the pan.*

★ *This recipe can also easily be halved if you want to make a smaller amount.*

100 g/3½ oz. Scotch bonnet peppers
1 bulb of garlic, cloves separated
  and peeled
5 g/1 teaspoon cloves
5 g/1 teaspoon pimento berries
1 large carrot, thickly sliced
1 large onion, quartered
100 ml/generous ⅓ cup white
  vinegar
25 ml/2 tablespoons soy sauce
175 g/6 oz. tomato ketchup
60 g/scant ½ cup plain/all-purpose
  flour
50 g/¼ cup demerara sugar

MAKES ABOUT 500 ML/2 CUPS

Place the Scotch bonnet peppers, garlic, cloves, pimento berries, carrot, onion, vinegar and soy sauce in a food processor or blender and blend until combined into a purée. Set aside until needed.

Put the ketchup with 125 ml/½ cup water in a saucepan and simmer over a low heat, whisking until combined. Add the blended pepper mixture, whisk together and continue to simmer over a low heat.

Use a sieve to sift in the flour, a little at a time, and whisk vigorously until the flour is fully combined with the sauce. Continue to simmer over a low heat for 20 minutes, whisking every 3–5 minutes.

After 20 minutes, whisk in the sugar, then leave to cool.

Store in the fridge in an airtight jar or bottle for up to a year – the flavours will intensify the longer it is kept.

BRIXTON-INSPIRED JERK SALT

You might have worked out by now that Caribbean cooking is a word-of-mouth gig. And by this, I mean that nothing is actually written down. We often learn these recipes from standing by our nan's side on a Sunday and then replicating them in our adulthood as we get older. No one can cook as good as Nan, but as the world evolves and cultures intertwine, you will find a host of the British-born Black generation elevating their at-home recipes for the modern palate. Visiting places like Pop Brixton or Boxpark in London, which house exciting culinary start-ups, you will easily find innovative thirty-something-year-old chefs remodelling what they know. The latest dish to have taken over the Caribbean market is jerk chips/fries for example. You might find them laced with cheese, pulled pork or made vegan with jackfruit. I always like to keep things simple, so this recipe aims to enhance any side dish and is my modern take on a traditional classic. Use an icing or salt shaker to spice up your meal as desired. Great for dusting over cooked chips, meat, fish and veg, hard food and works brilliantly with plantain.

60 g/2 oz. jerk powder
  (shop-bought, or see below
  for a homemade version)
30 g/1 oz. icing/powdered sugar
15 g/1 tablespoon table salt
large pinch of turmeric
6 g/1 tablespoon ground
  pimento berries

MAKES 100 G/3½ OZ.

Place all the ingredients in a food processor and pulse until combined. Transfer to an airtight container and store in a cool, dry place for up to 2 years.

HOMEMADE JERK POWDER
If you're unable to get hold of ready-made jerk powder, have a go at making your own:

10 g/2 teaspoons onion powder
10 g/2 teaspoons garlic powder
20 g/4 teaspoons dried chilli flakes/
  hot pepper flakes
20 g/4 teaspoons sea salt
20 g/4 teaspoons freshly ground
  black pepper
20 g/4 teaspoons dried thyme
20 g/4 teaspoons brown sugar
20 g/4 teaspoons ground
  pimento berries
10 g/2 teaspoons paprika
5 g/1 teaspoon ground cinnamon
pinch of ground nutmeg
pinch of ground cloves
10 g/2 teaspoons ground cumin

MAKES 150–200 G/5½–7 OZ.

Place all the ingredients in a food processor and pulse until combined. Use to season any meat or vegetables.

BBQ SAUCE

Nothing beats a good BBQ sauce. Growing up in Brixton, I would watch plumes of smoke billow from the barbecues/grills that were ever so carefully perched in front of local restaurants or in the gardens of people's homes. I would see goods like corn-on-the-cob, jackfruit, chicken or even fish being smoked to perfection and also being smothered in BBQ sauce.

And then to have opened my own restaurant, Paradise Cove and have our BBQ sauce requested frequently due to the amazing flavour it brings, makes me feel very proud. You just have to give this amazing sauce a go! Between you and me, I think it is the use of curry powder that makes it unique.

Once the BBQ sauce is on whatever you are cooking, just remember to keep the fire or heat low to get the best results as it stops the sugar scorching and will help to retain the most flavour.

200 ml/¾–1 cup tomato ketchup
200 g/1 cup sugar (ideally brown)
50 ml/scant ¼ cup soy sauce
50 ml/scant ¼ cup Worcestershire
   sauce
50 ml/scant ¼ cup sweet chilli sauce
1 tablespoon curry powder
   (for best results use Betapac
   Jamaican curry powder)
20 g/2⅓ tablespoons plain/
   all-purpose flour

MAKES ABOUT 500 ML/2 CUPS

Put all the ingredients, except the flour, in a saucepan over a high heat and whisk until combined. Sift in the flour and whisk until the sauce has thickened.

Leave to cool before serving, brushing onto your chosen ingredient or transfer to an airtight container and keep in the fridge for up to 4 weeks.

SIMPLE CARIBBEAN SALAD VINAIGRETTE

This is a recipe that I came up with when I was only 17 years old – so it's a Paradise Cove matriarch of sorts! It is packed with flavour and has stood the test of time. The key is to blend the onion as finely as possible and to mix the oil and vinegar correctly, so they emulsify and do not split.

3 teaspoons Dijon, English or
    wholegrain mustard
1 tablespoon Chef Tee's Simple Jerk
    Marinade (see page 16)
2 tablespoons icing/powdered sugar
1 teaspoon dried chilli flakes/hot
    pepper flakes
1 teaspoon freshly ground black
    pepper
½ red or white onion, chopped
15 g/½ oz. fresh thyme
150 ml/⅔ cup white vinegar
300 ml/1¼ cups vegetable oil

MAKES 500 ML/2 CUPS

Place the mustard, Jerk Marinade, icing sugar, dried chilli flakes, black pepper, onion and thyme in a food processor or blender and pulse for 30 seconds until combined and the onion is finely blended. If the blade sticks, add a little of the vinegar slowly, to help it keep moving.

Add the rest of the vinegar and pulse for a further 20 seconds. Leave the machine on auto and slowly pour the oil in as it keeps mixing – adding the oil too quickly will cause the mixture to split. Store in an airtight jar in the fridge for up to 6 weeks.

VARIATIONS You can use honey, maple syrup, agave or golden/corn syrup as a substitute for the icing sugar.

LEMON & CHILLI MAYONNAISE

Here is a recipe that I find goes well with a lot of the dishes that I have created for this book.

a splash of vegetable oil
5 garlic cloves, chopped
½ bunch of fresh thyme, sprigs
    snapped in half
½ teaspoon dried chilli flakes/hot
    pepper flakes (or more to taste)
grated zest and juice of 1 lemon
300 g/1½ cups mayonnaise
    (shop-bought or see below right
    for homemade)

MAKES ABOUT 400 ML/1⅔ CUPS

Heat the splash of oil in a cast-iron casserole dish/ Dutch oven over a high heat and sauté the garlic and thyme sprigs for a couple of minutes. Add the dried chilli flakes and continue to sauté for another minute until the garlic turns golden. Leave to cool to room temperature – this is important as a high heat will curdle the mayo.

Put the cooled garlic mixture, including the infused oil, in a food processor or blender and pulse for 20 seconds until the garlic mix is completely mashed.

Add the lemon zest and juice and pulse for about 4 seconds to combine. Add the mayonnaise and pulse again for about 5–10 seconds until combined.

For best results, store in an airtight container in the fridge for up to 1 month.

NOTE If the mayonnaise splits from overmixing, place the mixture in a bowl, then simply add an egg yolk and gently mix it in by hand. The proteins will help to bring the mixture back together.

HOMEMADE MAYONNAISE

If you don't have any pre-made mayonnaise to hand,
have a go at making your own.

Put 2 egg yolks and 1 tablespoon mustard in a food processor
or blender and pulse for 15 seconds. As it's mixing, slowly
add 150 ml/²/₃ cup vegetable, sunflower or olive oil through
the flue and continue mixing until the mayonnaise thickens.
Add a pinch of salt and black pepper and a pinch of turmeric.
Pulse again slowly, adding another 150 ml/²/₃ cup oil until
fully combined.

BITS & BITES

TO WHET YOUR APPETITE

My restaurant has been called 'a gentle journey around the Caribbean islands', and that is also a perfect way to describe this chapter. From Cuban-inspired green plantain fritters, to Jamaican bammy, to the all-encompassing plantain bites, here you will find a bit of everything to cook and nibble at.

These bites are great for small plates but can very easily be upscaled for large events, giving you the versatility to be either a Caribbean cook or a Caribbean chef.

Old zinc shed beside a mango tree in the countryside in Jamaica.

SIMPLE PLANTAIN WEDGES WITH MANGO SALSA

How could I not include a simple plantain recipe. Plantain is a staple in African and Caribbean cooking. It is a highly versatile fruit and can be served as a side, part of breakfast or with modern fusion dishes. People love it for its sweetness, soft texture and for its quick cooking ability. It is part of the banana family but unlike a banana it is firmer in feel. It also only develops its sweetness once cooked. Personal preferences make up a huge part of how plantain is cooked. My nan would take me to Electric Avenue in Brixton to choose the ripest ones. 'Black but not too black', she would say, with her preference for sweeter plantains. But my grandad, who had a stall in Hildreth street market, would prefer them yellow as they were not too sweet and great for boiling in soups.

Whatever your preference, have fun playing around with them, chopping them into different ways or cooking them with different methods. I have stylized them here, adding another piece of Caribbean gold – mango – but don't underestimate it. Nothing beats just simple good old fried plantain.

vegetable oil, for frying
3–4 ripe plantain, peeled and
    chopped into 2.5-cm/1-in. chunks
    (see Note below right)
Brixton-inpsired Jerk Salt
    (see page 26), for dusting (optional)

SALSA
½ mango, stoned/pitted, peeled
    and diced
½ red onion, diced
¼ Scotch bonnet pepper, finely diced
¼ bunch of fresh chives, snipped
2 fresh thyme sprigs, leaves removed
grated zest and juice of ½ lime

SERVES 2–4

First, make the salsa. Place all the ingredients in a bowl and mix everything together. Set aside for later.

Heat a shallow heavy-based saucepan with oil about 1–2 cm/½–¾ in. deep. Fry the plantain for 2 minutes for really ripe plantain and 4 minutes for less ripe plantain until golden all over. Be careful not to overcook them, as the plantain will continue to cook from the residual heat once removed from the pan. Remove from the pan with a slotted spoon and drain any excess oil on a plate lined with paper towels.

Serve the plantain wedges hot with the mango salsa and with an added dusting of Jerk Salt if liked.

NOTES

* *The ripe plantain should be yellow in colour with some black markings. Plantain that are too black are overripe.*

* *These wedges can also be deep-fried. Heat the oil to about 160–180°C/ 320–350°F on a thermometer. Otherwise, to check the oil is hot enough, flick a little water into the oil; if the oil spits back at you, it is hot enough to continue. When the wedges are golden, they are ready to serve.*

GREEN PLANTAIN FRITTERS

I came across this recipe a few years ago. It's not something that is usually considered Caribbean, as it is more commonly found in the Cuban islands, but it accompanies many meals perfectly. It's a tricky recipe to prepare – as green plantain skin can be hard to remove – but they work perfectly as a refreshing element to any meal.

2–4 green plantain, topped and tailed (see Note below right)
2–3 tablespoons garlic powder
1 teaspoon table salt
1 tablespoon freshly ground black pepper
vegetable oil, for frying

SERVES 4–6

Carefully run a knife down the back of the plantain, scoring the skin, then peel off the skin – this can be quite tricky. If the skin is quite hard, cut the skin off as though peeling potatoes. Grate the plantain into a bowl, cover with water and leave to soak for at least 20 minutes – but up to 3 hours for the best results – this helps to remove the starch. Drain the plantain through a sieve and pat dry to remove any excess liquid.

Place the plantain in a mixing bowl and add the garlic powder, salt and pepper. Don't be afraid to be heavy-handed with the garlic powder.

Loosely roll the seasoned, grated plantain into small 2.5-cm/1-in. sized balls. Be careful not to flatten the balls too much or roll them too tightly, or they will not cook in the centre.

Heat a shallow frying pan/skillet with oil about 4 cm/ 2½ in. deep. Fry the fritters for 10 minutes until they are golden brown and crispy all the way. Remove from the pan with a slotted spoon and drain any excess oil on a plate lined with paper towels.

Serve with hot sauce for dipping, if liked.

NOTES

★ *Please note that garlic granules or garlic salt will not work with this recipe. Garlic powder will give the best results as it dissolves easily.*

★ *Green plantain are also known as 'green' banana. It is important to use the correct type of plantain here as ripe plantain will not work.*

★ *These fritters can also be deep-fried. Heat the oil to about 160–180°C/ 320–350°F on a thermometer. Otherwise, to check the oil is hot enough, flick a little water into the oil; if the oil spits back at you, it is hot enough to continue. When the wedges are golden, they are ready to serve.*

PUMPKIN SOUP

Once upon a time, when I was 17, I worked in a small café in Balham and someone requested a pumpkin soup. I had a few herbs and spices, hot water and some veg and somehow came up with a quick and easy soup. I have altered the recipe as time has gone by, but have always loved its simplicity and versatility. More recently as I was writing this book, I had my wisdom tooth out and struggled to eat, so this dish was a staple for me, as it was quick and easy and light. Traditionally, pumpkin soup is made with Caribbean cock packs (a Caribbean soup seasoning). A stock is made, noodles are added as well as fresh sweetcorn, spinners (dumplings) and green bananas. However, for me the main star is, and will always be, the pumpkin.
My recipes are a guide, so feel free to add more or less of your favourite ingredient. When making this recipe you can create a chunkier texture with less blending. And to beef it up a bit, serve it with hard dough bread or roti (see page 88).

400 g/14 oz. pumpkin, peeled, deseeded and roughly chopped
2 red onions, quartered
1 red (bell) pepper, deseeded and roughly chopped
1 bulb of garlic, cloves separated
⅓ bunch of fresh thyme
olive oil, for drizzling
1 tablespoon good-quality vegetable bouillon or stock powder (I use Marigold vegetable stock powder)
100 ml/scant ½ cup hot water

TO SERVE
snipped fresh chives
créme fraîche
Jamaican hard dough bread or Trinidadian Bus Up Shut Roti (see page 88)

SERVES 4 AS AN APPETIZER
OR 2 AS A MAIN

Preheat the oven to 220°C fan/245°C/475°F/gas 9.

Place the pumpkin, onions and red pepper in a roasting tin.

Top and tail the garlic cloves, leaving the skin but remove the husk and stem. Crush each clove to release the flavour, and add to the tin.

Snap the thyme sprigs in half and throw over the veg mix. Drizzle olive oil over everything until all the vegetables are well coated, then add 50 ml/scant ¼ cup water.

Cover the roasting tin with foil, then roast in the preheated oven for 30–40 minutes until the pumpkin is soft and slightly charred.

Transfer the contents of the tin to a food processor or blender. Add the bouillon and the hot water. Blend until the soup reaches your desired consistency. For a thinner soup add more water (and bouillon if you wish), a little at a time.

Garnish with chives and serve with a swirl of crème fraîche and some Jamaican hard dough bread or roti.

JAMAICAN BAMMY

I discovered bammy when my aunty Annette introduced me to it early one morning. I caught her soaking the dried bread in milk, then frying it in a frying pan/skillet that looked like it had genuinely come from Jamaica. It was lovely – golden all round, crunchy on the outside and doughy on the inside. Making it takes skill but once mastered, it is a versatile dish that can be part of a breakfast or evening meal.

2 fresh cassava
light pinch of sea salt
light pinch of good-quality vegetable bouillon or stock powder (I use Marigold vegetable stock powder)
leaves from 1 fresh thyme sprig or 1 teaspoon Brixton-inspired Jerk Salt (see page 26) (optional)
30–50 ml/1–2 fl oz. vegetable oil

TO SOAK
250 ml/1 cup lukewarm water mixed with 1 teaspoon of good-quality vegetable bouillon or 1 x 400-g/ 14-oz. can of coconut milk

7–10 cm/3–4 in. diameter egg ring or heatproof circular cookie cutter

MAKES 4–6

Top and tail the cassava, then cut in half so you have 4 halves. Inspect the cassava before using – it should be white all the way through. Any signs of black or dark spots indicate rot, and these should be cut out or the cassava discarded. Stand the cassava up and use a sharp knife to cut away the skin. The cassava is firm in texture so take care doing this. Some remove the core – this is optional.

Put the cassava in a food processor and blend until it is mashed into a textured pulp. Place the pulp in a fine muslin cloth/cheesecloth or a loose woven cloth set over a sieve and gently squeeze the liquid out until the mixture is dry, creating a flour. Discard the liquid produced as this contains inedible starch.

Place the cassava flour in a bowl and season with the salt and bouillon. Add a generous sprinkle of fresh thyme leaves or Jerk Salt for a modern Caribbean inspired taste (if using) and mix well.

Heat the oil in a frying pan/skillet over a medium heat. Once hot, place an egg ring or heatproof circular cookie cutter in the pan and spoon in a couple of tablespoons of the seasoned cassava flour, forming it into a small disc about 1 cm/½ in. thick.

Cook in batches of 4 if you have a larger pan or 1–2 if you have a smaller pan. Fry the bammy for about 10–15 minutes, flipping halfway through, until lightly golden on both sides.

Set the bammy aside to cool, then soak in the seasoned water or coconut milk for 10–20 minutes.

Reheat the frying pan over a medium heat and fry the bammy again for about 3–4 minutes, flipping them over throughout cooking until golden brown on each side.

Serve with callaloo or a fish dish and enjoy!

NOTE *If not eating on the same day, the bammy can be frozen and used at a later date (defrost at room temperature, soak for a couple of hours, then reheat by frying).*

BEEF PATTIES

Patties... when they are done well, they are indescribably good, with a soft-textured, warm and buttery dough. You can be flexible with the filling but you have to get the dough right. If you don't do that, you will end up with a Cornish pasty-like pastry.

DOUGH

500 g/3¾ cups plain/all-purpose flour, plus extra for dusting

220 g/2 sticks butter or lard, cubed

1 heaped tablespoon turmeric

2 teaspoons caster/superfine sugar

1 heaped teaspoon curry powder

1 teaspoon sea salt

FILLING

splash of vegetable oil

½ onion, finely diced

2 garlic cloves, finely diced

20 g/¾ oz. fresh ginger, finely diced

½ bunch of spring onions/scallions, finely chopped

½ Scotch bonnet pepper, finely chopped

½ red (bell) pepper, deseeded and finely diced

1 x 198-g/7-oz. can of sweetcorn, drained

300–500 g/10½–1 lb. 2 oz. mince/ ground beef

1 tablespoon good-quality vegetable bouillon or stock powder (I use Marigold vegetable stock powder) or all-purpose seasoning

2 tablespoons garlic powder

1 teaspoon freshly ground black pepper

2 tablespoons dark soy sauce

2–4 tablespoons tomato purée/paste

2 tablespoons caster/superfine sugar

50 g/1 cup fresh breadcrumbs (optional)

MAKES 6–8

To make the dough, place the ingredients in a bowl and mix together firmly using your hands until it starts to resemble breadcrumbs. Alternatively, you can mix in a food processor for the quickest results. Slowly add 250–300 ml/1–1¼ cups water, a little at a time, until the mixture forms a dough.

Sprinkle a surface heavily with flour and roll the dough out into a rectangular shape. Fold the dough in half and roll it out flat again. Repeat this step 4 more times. Wrap the dough in cling film/plastic wrap and chill in the fridge for 1–2 hours.

Meanwhile, to make the filling, heat a splash of oil in a frying pan/skillet over a medium heat and sauté the onion, garlic, ginger, spring onions, Scotch bonnet pepper, red pepper and sweetcorn for about 10 minutes until starting to soften. Add the beef and continue to cook over a medium heat, breaking up the meat as you stir. Add the remaining filling ingredients and the breadcrumbs, if using, and cook until the meat is brown in colour all the way through. Set the filling mixture aside to cool for when the dough is ready.

Preheat the oven to 170°C fan/190°C/375°F/gas 5. Line a baking sheet with non-stick baking paper.

Once the dough has chilled, roll it out on a lightly floured surface to about 3mm/⅛ in. thick. Use a large breakfast bowl (about 16 cm/6 in. in diameter) to cut out circles from the dough – you should get about 6–8 circles. Set these aside for filling.

Place 1–2 heaped tablespoons of the filling mixture in the centre of each dough circle. Rub a little water on the curved edge of the case. Fold the dough circle over so that the edges meet – it should look like a semi-circle shape with filling inside – and press it closed with your finger. Indent the sealed edges with a fork, creating the signature patty finish. Place the patties on the lined baking sheet and bake in the preheated oven for 20–30 minutes until golden.

NOTE *Minced beef is generally chunkier than typical patty filling texture, so for a finer texture, once cooked, add the mix to a food processor and pulse for 4 seconds. Scrape the sides down and pulse again.*

JERK WINGS WITH STICKY RUM SAUCE

I have seen street food parks become popular over the last few years, and chicken wings in particular have really blown up in popularity. Wings = Creativity. So to all my chicken wing chefs, this recipe is my Caribbean-inspired nod to those battling it out in the street food markets. PS, vegans can swap the meat out for jackfruit.

500 g/1 lb. 2 oz. chicken wings
  (see Note)
30 g/1 oz. Greek yogurt
60 g/2 oz. Chef Tee's Simple Jerk
  Marinade (see page 16)
½ bunch of fresh thyme,
  leaves removed

STICKY RUM SAUCE
4 garlic cloves, peeled
¼ onion, peeled
50–100 g/¼–½ cup granulated
  sugar
100 ml/3½ fl oz. tomato ketchup
75 ml/⅓ cup malt brown vinegar
50 ml/scant ¼ cup dark soy sauce
50 ml/3 tablespoons honey
1 teaspoon English mustard
1–2 tablespoons good-quality
  cornflour or plain/all-purpose flour
125 ml/½ cup white rum

TO SERVE
baby leaf spinach
pineapple chunks
roasted peppers
snipped fresh chives

SERVES 2–4

Preheat the oven to 220°C fan/245°C/475°F/gas 9.

Place the meat in a small roasting tin and rub all over with the yogurt. Cover the tin and place in the fridge for 15–20 minutes – this process helps to tenderize the meat, as the acidity from the yogurt helps break down the proteins; it can be skipped if you are short on time though.

Remove the tin from the fridge and season the wings vigorously with the Jerk Marinade and thyme by rubbing them into the skin. Add about 60 ml/¼ cup water to the tin – the steam helps the wings cook faster and stops the base of the tin scorching – and cover the roasting tin tightly with foil. Bake in the preheated oven for 20 minutes, or until the wings begin to scorch.

Meanwhile, make the sauce. Put the garlic, onion, sugar and 125ml/½ cup water in a food processor and pulse until combined. Transfer to a saucepan. Add the ketchup, soy sauce, honey, mustard and cornflour and combine with a whisk. Bring to the boil and continue boiling until the sauce thickens. If the sauce is too thin, add a little more cornflour; if it is too thick add a little more water. Leave the sauce to cool.

After 20 minutes roasting, drain the cooking juices from the wings and add this stock and the rum to the cooled sauce and whisk together.

Pour the sauce generously over the wings, saving some sauce for serving. Cover the roasting tin with foil and return to the oven for a further 10 minutes, then remove the foil and roast the wings, uncovered, for a final 10 minutes until slightly charred.

Serve the chicken wings, alongside any leftover sauce, on a bed of fresh spinach leaves with pineapple, roasted peppers and garnish with chives.

NOTE *To prepare the chicken wings for cooking, I like to burn the hairs off using the fire from a gas stove, then wash them in water with a little vinegar or lime juice.*

FISH & SEAFOOD DISHES

STEAMED, GRILLED & FRIED

Jamaica in particular is famous for its fish dishes, which makes sense with its national dish being ackee and saltfish. Fish and seafood, such as lobster, snapper, sea bream, sea bass, prawns/shrimps, saltfish and rainbow fish are easily found and can be baked, grilled/broiled, roasted, sautéed or steamed – the possibilities here are really endless.

Aside from saltfish, which is salted cod, the Caribbean is mostly known for its use of snapper. Snapper is commonly fried or barbecued, it has a delicate texture but is often known to be full of bones. For those unfamiliar with this fish, it can be tricky, so feel free to swap it for a fish that you are more comfortable handling. This section includes a range of recipes to get you started and give you a gentle introduction to Caribbean fish cookery.

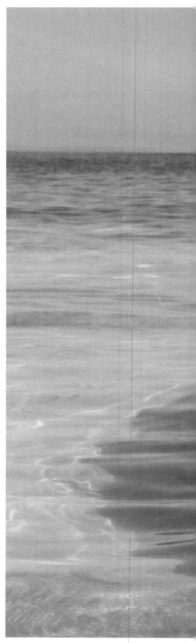

Above left: Red snapper at the fish market.
Above right: An old fishing boat docked near
Labadee, Haiti.

ACKEE & SALTFISH

Ackee and saltfish is interestingly Jamaica's national dish, not the commonly thought jerk chicken. What many don't recognize is this dish has its history deeply rooted in slavery. Ackee originates from parts of Africa and was eaten on slave ships alongside the dried salted (cod) fish. It was salted to help preserve it for long journeys. The story varies depending on where it is heard, but the two elements eventually combine to create the dish we know and love.

In recent years ackee has soared in popularity, but the most humble pairing will always be with saltfish. Ackee I describe like scrambled egg, just lighter in texture. The final advice I would give, is to add the ackee last and not 'mash it'. Folding the ackee gently helps it keep its shape.

300 g/10½ oz. skinned and boneless saltfish (1 pack)
50 ml/3½ tablespoons vegetable oil
1 red (bell) pepper, chopped
1 yellow (bell) pepper, chopped
1 large onion, chopped
1 bunch of spring onions/scallions, chopped and white and green parts separated
1 Scotch bonnet pepper, chopped
½ bunch of fresh thyme sprigs
1½ tablespoons good-quality vegetable bouillon or stock powder (I use Marigold vegetable stock powder)
1 teaspoon freshly ground black pepper
1 teaspoon icing/powdered sugar
1 x 540-g/19-oz. can of ackee, drained then washed in hot water

SERVES 4

Completely cover the saltfish with water in a saucepan and boil over a high heat until a foam residue forms on the surface of the water. Be careful as the water can easily boil over the pan. Drain the fish and return to the pan with fresh water. Complete this boiling and draining process twice more. This is essential to rehydrate the fish and to remove the salt. The fish should be flaky once finished. It should still taste salty but not unbearably so. Set the drained fish aside.

Heat the oil in a saucepan over a high heat. Add the peppers, onion, white parts of the spring onions and Scotch bonnet pepper and sauté until it all begins to soften. If the vegetables begin to stick, add a small amount of water.

Snap the thyme sprigs in half and add to the pan. After a few minutes, turn the heat to medium and add the saltfish, bouillon, black pepper and sugar, stirring it all together to create a stock and well-seasoned saltfish mix.

Add the ackee to the pan, carefully folding it in. Sauté gently, taking care not to mash the ackee. Add the green spring onions at the end to give colour and serve straight away.

FOIL-BAKED CURRIED PRAWNS

Later in the book, you can find curry recipes that you could easily adapt for prawns/shrimp (by swapping the meat for seafood) but I wanted to do something slightly different here.

Caribbean cuisine isn't really hard. In fact it is generally very unfussy and simplistic. However, the moment a chef deviates away from what we know, we often face a backlash from people and are accused of 'diluting the authenticity'. We have very little freedom and flexibility. For me, the truth is your food is only as authentic as you are, and I proudly take inspiration from my own story... I wanted to expand my fish menu but didn't know how to do it. My kitchen is small and I adamantly didn't want another curry. One day I had a look at what my friend was doing (as you do from time to time to seek inspiration from others) and then remembered about cooking fish 'en papillote'. I tested out a range of cooking different things in foil and, with a bit of creativity, I ended up with foil-baked curried prawns.

I absolutely love this cooking method. It's foolproof. Just go easy on the optional ingredients and be sure the curry powder is well blended and cooked out.

NOTE Okra and spinach can also be added to the foil parcel to cook with the prawns if liked.

1 large onion, roughly chopped
1 bunch of spring onions/scallions
2½ tablespoons curry powder (for best results use Betapac Jamaican curry powder)
1 tablespoon good-quality vegetable bouillon or stock powder (I use Marigold vegetable stock powder)
25 g/1 oz. granulated sugar
2 teaspoons English mustard (optional)
2 cloves (optional)
1 kg /2¼ lb. large prawns/shrimp, shelled with tails left intact if possible
30 ml/2 tablespoons vegetable oil
1 lime, halved

SERVES 4–6

Preheat the oven to 225°C fan/245°C/475°F/gas 9. Place a large piece of foil in a roasting tin – large enough that it can be folded over the prawns to make a parcel.

Place the onion, spring onions, curry powder, bouillon, sugar and mustard and cloves, if using, in a food processor with 200 ml/generous ¾ cup water. Pulse until the mixture forms a paste. If the food processor blades stick, add more water, a little at a time, until a wet paste is formed.

Place the prawns in a mixing bowl and add the blended paste, stirring together so the prawns are well coated.

Tip the prawns out onto the lined roasting tin. Drizzle the prawns with the oil, squeeze over the lime juice and add the lime halves to the tin. Fold over the foil and press the edges together to seal the prawns in a parcel. Roast in the preheated oven for 10–20 minutes until the praws are pink all the way through. Serve.

COCONUT, GARLIC & THYME PRAWNS

Interestingly coconut isn't one of my favourite flavours, but my friend Lara would never forgive me for not including it in one of her favourite dishes. I can tell you Lara and I have spent years trying prawns together – sometimes even driving from London to Brighton or other parts of the country after work to get the dish. We love prawns!

From much practice, we have learned that when it comes to prawns, the key is to not cook them for too long and to not overseason them. Me and Lara would both agree that the easiest prawns are shell-off, tail-on, but for those who want a little bit of extra flavour, keep the full shell on.

thumb-sized piece of fresh ginger
1 large onion, roughly chopped
grated zest of 1 lime
6–8 garlic cloves, to taste, peeled
½ x 400-ml/14-oz. can of coconut milk
10 g/⅓ oz. fresh thyme sprigs
1 bunch of spring onions/scallions, topped and tailed
25 g/1 oz. granulated sugar
1 kg/2¼ lb. large prawns/shrimp, shelled with tails left intact if possible
30–50 ml/2–3½ tablespoons vegetable oil

TO SERVE
salad leaves
chopped grilled pineapple
lime wedges

SERVES 4–6

Place all of the ingredients, except the prawns and the oil, in a food processor with 100 ml/generous ⅓ cup water and pulse until the mixture forms a paste. If the blades stick, add some water, a little at a time, until a wet paste is formed.

Put the prawns in a mixing bowl and add the blended paste. Mix well so the prawns are well coated.

Heat a shallow griddle pan/ridged stove-top grill pan with the oil over a high heat. To test if the oil is hot, flick water into the pan and if it spits the water back, you will know it's the correct temperature.

Griddle the prawns for about 5–10 minutes until pink and slightly charred in colour. Serve on a bed of mixed salad leaves, garnished with some grilled pineapple and lime wedges.

BAKED SNAPPER STUFFED WITH CALLALOO, LIME & OKRA

My aunt Julie is famous in Brixton for her parties. I don't know anyone else who could cordon off a road, every year, just for her Easter party. But for the past 10 years, what started as just a family gathering, has become a yearly Easter event involving over 100 people and the entire road. I man the barbecue each year, and make sauces or cakes, while adults dance and children Easter egg hunt. Little meat is eaten with Good Friday having just passed, so we make do with a range of fish dishes. Tuna pasta with sweet chilli sauce, fried sprats, ackee and saltfish and this recipe she taught me, which was most likely passed down from her mum (aunty Annette). It's a really simple dish, and one that broadens your foil-baking skills. These two women are pretty influential in my life. They taught me a lot more than just how to cook, which perhaps explains why this dish is on the menu at Paradise Cove.

30 ml/2 tablespoons vegetable oil

1 x 540-g/19-oz can of callaloo (or substitute with fresh spinach or kale), washed and drained

1–2 tablespoons Brixton-inspired Jerk Salt (see page 26), good-quality vegetable bouillon or stock (I use Marigold vegetable stock powder) or all-purpose seasoning

2–4 snapper fish, gutted and scored, with the head and fins still intact (each weighing about 200–350 g/ 7–12½ oz.)

2–4 tablespoons Chef Tee's Simple Jerk Marinade (see page 16)

a few pinches of caster/superfine sugar

½ onion, sliced into rings

8–16 okra (allow 4 per fish)

½ bulb of garlic, sliced widthways to expose the cloves inside

1 Scotch bonnet pepper, roughly chopped

olive oil, for drizzling

½ lime

SERVES 2–4

Preheat the oven to 160°C fan/180°C/350°F/gas 4.

Heat the oil in a pan over a high heat and lightly sauté the callaloo with the Jerk Salt, bouillon powder or all-purpose seasoning for about 10 minutes. Set aside to cool down.

Rub the Jerk Marinade and a pinch of sugar vigorously into each fish, making sure they are coated evenly and the seasoning is rubbed into the scored skin and insides.

Roll out a large amount of foil (triple the size of the fish) and lay the fish in the centre. Stuff the cavity of each fish with the sautéed callaloo.

Top the fish with the onion, okra, garlic and Scotch bonnet pepper, drizzle with olive oil and squeeze over the lime juice, leaving the lime husk inside the foil. Add a little extra seasoning of your choice to the veg if you wish.

Wrap the fish in the foil to make a parcel and place in a roasting tin – not too tight otherwise the skin will stick, or too loose as the juices will leak out. Bake in the preheated oven for 30–40 minutes. You can tell the fish is cooked when the flesh pulls easily away from the bones and is white and flaky.

Serve with steamed rice or hard dough bread.

SALTFISH FRITTERS

Saltfish fritters is one of my oldest recipes. Once you pick up the knack for making a batter you can create quite a lot – banana fritters, plantain fritters, coconut fritters, etc. The key is the water to flour ratio, which should be roughly 1:2. This is the ratio for all my fritters and no egg or baking powder is needed.

There are a few components to get right. The first is to make sure the saltfish is boiled out correctly to help keep the balance of flavour. The second is to make sure that you sauté the veg first – if you don't do that the raw veg may leak too much moisture into the batter. And the third is leaving the mixture for at least 4 hours to let the gluten develop. You could use the batter straight away but this will just lead to a shorter texture. However, this recipe can be made with a gluten-free flour, as long as it is a high-quality one, in which case you can use the batter straight away.

300 g/10½ oz. skinned and boneless
   saltfish (1 pack)
2 green (bell) peppers, chopped
2 yellow (bell) peppers, chopped
1 bunch of spring onions/scallions,
   trimmed and chopped, green
   and white parts separated
½ bunch of fresh thyme sprigs
vegetable oil, for frying
1 teaspoon ground black pepper
2 tablespoons good-quality
   vegetable bouillon or stock
   powder (I use Marigold vegetable
   stock powder)
600 g/4½ cups self-raising/
   self-rising flour
140 g/scant ¾ cup granulated sugar
1 tablespoon turmeric or curry
   powder (for best results use
   Betapac Jamaican curry powder)

TO SERVE
lemon wedges
Lemon and Chilli Mayonnaise
   (see page 30)

MAKES ABOUT 1 KG/2¼ LB. BATTER (SERVES
ANYTHING FROM 6–16 PEOPLE DEPENDING
ON WHAT SIZE YOU MAKE THE FRITTERS!)

Follow the instructions on page 52 for boiling the saltfish to remove the salt and prepare it for cooking.

Place the peppers, white parts of the spring onions and the thyme in a food processor and pulse to a chunky paste.

Heat a little oil in a pan over a medium heat and sauté the pulsed veg and the prepared saltfish with the black pepper and bouillon for about 10 minutes, stirring well. Once done, remove from the heat and leave to cool to room temperature.

Place the flour, sugar, turmeric and 450 ml/scant 2 cups water in a large bowl with the green parts of the spring onions and mix together to a batter. Add the sautéed saltfish and mix together to create a sticky batter. If you have time, rest the batter in the fridge overnight for best results.

Heat a shallow pan with oil to about 160°C/320°F if you have a thermometer. Otherwise, to check the oil is hot enough, flick a little water into the oil; if the oil spits back at you, it is hot enough to continue. Spoon the mixture in, a spoonful at a time, and fry the fritters, in batches if needed, for 4–6 minutes until golden brown all over. Be careful not to fry the fritters on too high a heat as this will cook the outside only and leave a raw batter inside.

Enjoy the fritters with lemon wedges and Lemon and Chilli Mayonnaise for dipping, if liked.

NOTE *These fritters can also be deep-fried; when they float to the top, they are ready.*

JERK SEA BASS

Snapper, rainbow trout, sea bream, saltfish and squid are all favourites of the Caribbean, particularly snapper. However, snapper is notorious for its many bones. For me, my preference has been, and will always be, for sea bass. I am a pretty modern guy and like things easy, and sea bass is a much easier fish to manage. It also generally requires less seasoning.

You will really have to approach this recipe with your chef's hat on in order to gauge what is the best amount of seasoning to use. My marinade is different to shop-bought marinade, and depending on the time of the year, Scotch bonnet peppers are hotter, which creates more variables. In essence what I am trying to say is, you can easily under- or over-season your sea bass fillets. With that in mind, try to do what I do and give the fillets a translucent, even coating of marinade. That way you're less likely to have pockets of fish that aren't seasoned correctly.

2 x sea bass fillets, pin-boned and
   filleted (weighing about 120–180 g/
   4½–6 oz. each)
2 tablespoons Chef Tee's Simple Jerk
   Marinade (see page 16)
1 teaspoon desiccated/dried
   shredded coconut
30 ml/2 tablespoons vegetable oil
a few fresh thyme sprigs
juice of ½ lime

TO SERVE
salad leaves
Lemon and Chilli Mayonnaise
   (see page 30)

SERVES 2

Check the sea bass fillets and remove any additional bones you find. Rub the Jerk Marinade and desiccated coconut all over the fillets to give a translucent, even coating.

Heat the oil in a shallow pan over a high heat to about 160°C/325°F if you have a thermometer. Otherwise, to check the oil is hot enough, flick a little water into the oil; if the oil spits back at you, it is hot enough to continue. Carefully lay the thyme sprigs in the pan and then lay the sea bass fillets, skin-side down, on top – this will ensure you get a crispy skin. When the fish begins to turn white, squeeze the lime juice over the top. You can flip the fish fillets, however it is best to leave it on one side during cooking to keep it intact.

Once the sea bass is fully cooked, after about 10 minutes, use a spatula to carefully lift it out of the pan and transfer to a serving plate. Serve with salad leaves and Lemon and Chilli Mayonnaise or Kale, Cabbage and Callaloo (see page 128) and plain rice.

JERK SNAPPER WITH A PINEAPPLE & LIME SALAD

While on holiday in Jamaica, I was exposed to so many dishes but I also really got to know 'jerk'. The signature is the taste of pimento wood used on the drum or the pimento berries used in the marinade. Jerk varies in saltiness and spice but pimento is the key. I tried many barbecued foods while in Jamaica, and it made me wonder what side dishes would bring a cooling contrast to the acidity of the smoke in the barbecued dish. So, back home in London I began experimenting with fruits and a simple salad. I have chosen pineapple and lime (which is more commonly used in the Caribbean than lemon) but roasted pepper and apple also worked too.

3 tablespoons Chef Tee's Simple Jerk Marinade (see page 16)
2–4 snapper fish, gutted and scored, with the head and fins still intact (each fish weighing about 200–350 g/7–12½ oz.)
60 g/2 oz. fresh thyme

PINEAPPLE & LIME SALAD
1 cos/Romaine lettuce, chopped
1 red onion, chopped
1 x 213-g/8-oz. can of pineapple chunks, drained
olive oil, for drizzling
juice of 1 lime
1 small jar of roasted tomatoes, drained

TO SERVE
Escovitch Sauce (see page 67)
white rice

SERVES 2–4

Place the Jerk Marinade in a bowl. Coat each fish vigorously with the marinade, making sure they are coated evenly and the seasoning is rubbed into the scored skin and insides. Divide the thyme sprigs between the fish and stuff them inside the cavity of each one.

Heat a barbecue or griddle pan/ridged stove-top grill pan to a high heat with a little oil.

Cook the fish, turning carefully every few minutes, for about 15–20 minutes until the fish has a nice crust, flakes easily and is cooked through.

Meanwhile, prepare the salad by arranging the lettuce leaves, onion and pineapple on a serving platter with generous helpings of olive oil, lime juice and roasted tomatoes.

Serve the fish with the salad, a helping of Escovitch Sauce and white rice.

CLASSIC FRIED FISH WITH ESCOVITCH SAUCE

My grandad was a Rastafarian (meaning his diet was plant-based or pescetarian), and this dish was one of his specialities. One of the strongest memories I have of him, is him eating this fried fish and carefully picking out the bones of the snapper fillet. Fish was something my grandad did, and knew how to do well. His escovitch sauce never tasted shop-bought and it always had the kick of Scotch bonnet. So if you're making this dish, be brave and go for a bit of extra heat. My grandad always added an extra Scotch bonnet and it was one of the best things he ever did.

15 g/1 tablespoon garlic salt

15 g/1 tablespoon crushed pimento berries

15 g/1 tablespoon finely ground black pepper

60 g/½ cup plain/all-purpose flour

60 g/2 oz. Brixton-inspired Jerk Salt (see page 26) or other good-quality fish seasoning

⅓ bunch of fresh thyme

½ bulb of garlic, cloves crushed

50–100 ml/¼–⅓ cup vegetable oil

2 x snapper fish (sea bream or sea bass can also be used), gutted and scored, with the head and fins still intact (each weighing about 200–350 g/7–12½ oz.)

ESCOVITCH SAUCE

1 large onion, sliced into rings (use red onion for added colour)

1 carrot, cut into thin slices

1 red (bell) pepper, cut into rings

5 g/1 teaspoon cloves (optional)

¼ bunch of fresh thyme

1–2 Scotch bonnet peppers, diced

1 teaspoon crushed pimento berries

150–200 ml/⅔–¾ cup white wine vinegar

SERVES 2

Place the garlic salt, pimento berries, black pepper, flour, Jerk Salt, thyme and garlic in a bowl and mix together.

Coat each fish with this dry seasoning, making sure they are coated evenly and the seasoning is rubbed into the scored skin and insides. Save any leftover seasoning in the bowl and set aside.

Heat the oil in a frying pan/skillet over a high heat until it reaches around 180°c/350°F on a thermometer. Otherwise, to check the oil is hot enough, flick a little water into the oil; if the oil spits back at you, it is hot enough to continue. Carefully place the fish in the oil to shallow-fry for a few minutes, then turn them over to fry until slightly golden; this should take no more than 10 minutes in total.

Carefully remove the fish from the pan and re-coat it in the dry seasoning for extra flavour. Fry the fish again for 10–15 minutes until it is crispy on each side. Remove it from the pan and let it rest on paper towels to drain any excess oil.

To make the escovitch, in the same pan you fried the fish, pour out the excess oil. Turn the heat to high and add the onion, carrot and pepper. Sauté for 5 minutes, adding back some of the oil if needed. Add the remaining ingredients and turn the heat to low. Leave the veg to simmer and infuse with the vinegar for 3 minutes, then take off the heat.

Dress the fish with the escovitch pickled veg and drizzle with some extra vinegar for added sharpness. Serve with white rice, steamed veg, callaloo or Jamaican Bammy (see page 43).

NOTE *Escovitch sauce is classically made with white onions, but I have used red onions. People say red onions are just for salads, but I find they have a slightly sweeter, more intense taste and work just as well.*

PLANT-BASED ITAL DISHES

A RASTAFARIAN WAY OF EATING

When I first opened Paradise Cove in 2020, I really had no idea
what we would become.

On a hot July day as I was making the signs, I bumped into
my neighbour Sabrina. With a 2-m./6.5-ft. distance, as prescribed
by lockdown, we introduced ourselves and soon after opening,
she came down with her boyfriend Adam to try us out! Now, I had
always been familiar with ital food as a Rastafarian way of living,
and therefore already knew of a few good plant-based dishes, but
it wasn't until meeting Sabrina, Adam and their family on regular
restaurant visits, that I really began to explore the endless
possibilities that plant-based dishes have to offer.

We did incredibly well as a restaurant and, less than a year after
opening, I developed and opened a second vegan branch! This lead
me to explore a range of ital dishes and push myself further.

Although I am not vegan myself, it's thanks to the requests of
Sabrina and Adam that I explored a range of dishes, which are
here in this chapter for you to try, too. This chapter is dedicated
to Sabrina and Alex – thank you for being part of my story.

*Tropical Caribbean landscape
of the island of Antigua.*

CLASSIC HARD FOOD WITH BUTTERED CABBAGE

Some of my recipes have a modern twist, but some things you just cannot improve on. Hard food is one of them. I love hard food. There is something very nourishing about it. I first came across this dish when I was a child and living in Balham. Collectively we would all take turns at sneakily picking more food from the pot, even after we had eaten... Only because it tasted so good! Sneaking food from the pot is a bit of a tradition. Feel free to use lashings of butter with your cabbage and I would strongly advise to add chocho/chayote if you can find it. It is simply delicious.

300 g/2¼ cups plain/all-purpose
    flour
100 g/²/₃ cup cornmeal/polenta
1 teaspoon table salt
1–2 green plantain, topped and tailed
    scored lengthways with a knife on
    one side
½ yellow yam, peeled and chopped
    into 5-cm/2-in. pieces

BUTTERED CABBAGE
50 ml/scant ¼ cup vegetable oil
1 white or Savoy cabbage,
    finely shredded
2 chocho/chayote, cored, peeled
    and thinly sliced
1 carrot, thinly sliced
1 red (bell) pepper, thinly sliced
1 onion, thinly sliced
1 tomato, chopped (optional)
1 Scotch bonnet pepper, finely
    chopped (optional)
1 teaspoon garlic powder or 30 g/
    1 oz. freshly grated garlic
1 teaspoon ground black pepper
¼ bunch of fresh thyme
60 g/¼ cup plant-based butter,
    plus more to taste if needed

SERVES 4–8 (DEPENDING ON WHO
GETS TO THE POT FIRST!)

First, make the buttered cabbage. Heat the oil in a large saucepan over a medium heat. Add the cabbage and chocho and sauté for a couple of minutes until they start to sweat. Add the carrot, pepper, onion and tomato and Scotch bonnet (if using) and continue to sauté. If it starts to stick, turn the heat to low and add a little water to loosen the mixture.

Add the garlic powder, black pepper, thyme and butter. Reduce the heat to low, cover the pot and leave the vegetables to steam for up to 15 minutes, stirring the mix every couple of minutes. When finished, add more butter to taste if needed. Set aside until ready to serve.

Begin making the hard foods. Put the flour, cornmeal and salt in a large bowl with 200 ml/generous ¾ cup water and mix together, being careful not to overwork the mixture or it will become tight from the gluten being over mixed.

Bring a large saucepan of salted water to the boil. Keep the lid on and reduce the heat to medium to keep the water at a rolling boil.

Roll small, palm-sized pieces of the dough into balls, then press flat. Place the dumplings in the pan of boiling water. Add the plantain and yams and boil for 20–30 minutes. Turn the heat off when the dumplings are cooked and the skin has slightly opened on the green plantain. The dumplings will be firm and cooked all the way through and have a soft and chewy texture if you bite them or split them with a fork. The water will have a slightly grey colour at this point, which is caused by the iron from the plantain discolouring the water.

Serve the dumplings, yams and plantain with the buttered cabbage (reheat it if necessary). Hard food is best consumed within 24 hours.

NOTE *Yellow yams are more common to the Caribbean, whereas white yams are more common to African regions.*

CHICKPEA MEDLEY

In recent years, the chickpea has become a popular ingredient for those who wish to adopt a vegan diet. It is great for a range of dishes, including curries, and this recipe is one of my most popular. What makes this great is the added use of raisins and coconut milk – which you can omit, however, for me they both bring a sweet creaminess to the dish which is delicious to eat.

30 ml/2 tablespoons vegetable oil

1 teaspoon dried chilli flakes/
   hot pepper flakes

thumb-sized piece of fresh ginger,
   peeled and grated

½ garlic clove, crushed

1 teaspoon ground black pepper

1 tablespoon paprika

2 tablespoons turmeric

50 g/¼ cup granulated sugar

1–2 onions, roughly chopped
   (about 200 g/2 oz.)

⅓ bunch of fresh thyme

2 x 400-g/14-oz cans of chickpeas/
   garbanzo beans, washed and
   drained

½ x 400-g/14-oz can of coconut milk
   or creamed coconut block

2 tablespoons good-quality
   vegetable bouillon or stock
   powder (I use vegan Marigold
   vegetable stock powder), plus
   extra if needed

150 g/5½ oz. pumpkin, peeled,
   deseeded and cut into chunks

50 g/⅓ cup raisins or sultanas/
   golden raisins

1 red (bell) pepper, chopped

TO SERVE
Perfectly Steamed Rice
   (see page 123)
wilted spinach and grated carrots

SERVES 6–8

Heat the oil in a large saucepan over a high heat. Add the dried chilli flakes, ginger, garlic, black pepper, paprika, turmeric and sugar and mix to make a paste. Add the onion and thyme and sauté for a few minutes only. If the onions start to catch on the bottom of the pan, add a little water to loosen it and reduce the heat. You will want a thick paste before adding the rest of the ingredients.

Add the chickpeas to the pan and stir well so the seasoning is evenly distributed. Add the coconut milk, bouillon, pumpkin, raisins and red pepper, along with 400 ml/1¾ cups water and simmer over a medium heat for about 30 minutes until thickened and the pumpkin is soft.

Taste to check the flavouring and add more bouillon, a teaspoon at a time, if necessary. Serve with steamed rice, wilted spinach and grated carrots.

SWEETCORN FRITTERS

The more time I have spent cooking, the more conscious I have become of what I am eating, and these fritters are a product of that. I remember thinking to myself, how could I make traditional saltfish fritters vegan? I then remembered my friend Lara who told me of her trying sweetcorn fritters at a restaurant on Streatham Hill. At first I tried many other meat substitutes but, for me, the corn added a sweet balance to my batter with an amazing fried crunch. My preference for these fritters is to deep-fry them as this perfects a soft doughy texture (even with gluten free flour) but if shallow frying... just merely be patient, as this has the same result.

500 g/3¾ cups self-raising/
   self-rising flour
75 g/⅓ cup granulated sugar
½ tablespoon curry powder
   (for best results use Betapac
   Jamaican curry powder)
½ tablespoon turmeric
½ teaspoon freshly ground
   black pepper
1 small can of sweetcorn, drained
   (about 150 g/5½ oz.)
1 red (bell) pepper, deseeded
   and roughly chopped
1 bunch of spring onions/scallions,
   roughly chopped
½ bunch of fresh thyme
1 tablespoon good-quality vegetable
   bouillon or stock powder
   (I use vegan Marigold vegetable
   stock powder)
200 ml/generous ¾ cup lukewarm
   water
vegetable oil, for frying

MAKES 16–20 FRITTERS

Place the flour, sugar, curry powder, turmeric, black pepper and sweetcorn in a large mixing bowl.

Put the red pepper, spring onions and thyme sprigs in a food processor and pulse for 8 seconds. Scrape the sides down, then pulse again. Add this mixture to the bowl of flour and sweetcorn.

Mix the bouillon with the lukewarm water in a jug/pitcher until dissolved, then add to the sweetcorn mixture. Stir everything together to make a thick, lumpy batter.

Heat a little oil in a shallow pan to about 160°C/325°F if you have a thermometer. Otherwise, to check the oil is hot enough, flick a little water into the oil; if the oil spits back at you, it is hot enough to continue.

Add a tablespoonful of batter at a time to the pan and fry the fritters, in batches if needed, for 3–4 minutes, turning halfway through, until golden brown all over. Be careful not to fry the fritters on too high a heat as this will cook the outside and leave a raw batter inside. Place the fritters on paper towels to drain any excess oil, then serve straightaway.

NOTE *These can also be deep-fried; when the fritters float to the top, they are cooked.*

MARTINIQUE-STYLE VEG

I have always said that Paradise Cove is a story (see page 6), and once upon a time when I was cooking from home, all my little orders had custom-made, collectable recipe cards to encourage you to cook at home. This recipe was one of them. Feel free to edit the vegetables as you see fit and serve with any classic Caribbean dish.

2 large carrots, peeled and cut into thick slices

75 g/2¾ oz. butternut squash, peeled, deseeded and cut into wedges

2 parsnips, peeled and cut into chunks

175 g/6 oz. Maris Piper potatoes, peeled and cut into wedges

2 chocho/chayote, cored, peeled and thickly sliced

1 red (bell) pepper, deseeded and thickly sliced

1 large onion, thickly sliced

1 large red onion, thickly sliced

1–2 sweet potatoes, peeled and cut into bite-sized chunks

1 lemon, halved

1 lime, halved

⅓ bunch of fresh thyme

1 bulb of garlic, cloves separated and crushed

5 okra, topped and tailed

30 g/2 tablespoons granulated sugar

15 g/1 tablespoon freshly ground black pepper

15 g/1 tablespoon coarse sea salt

15 g/1 tablespoon Brixton-inspired Jerk Salt (see page 26) or 30 g/ 2 tablespoons shop-bought jerk seasoning

30 g/2 tablespoons good-quality vegetable bouillon or stock powder (I use vegan Marigold vegetable stock powder)

75 ml/⅓ cup olive or vegetable oil

SERVES 4–6

Preheat the oven to 180°C fan/200°C/400°F/gas 6.

Place all of the vegetables in a large saucepan and cover with water. Bring to the boil and cook for 20 minutes over a medium heat until al dente. Drain the vegetables and blanch in cold water before transferring to a large roasting tin.

Add the lemon and lime halves, thyme sprigs, garlic and okra. Sprinkle over the sugar, black pepper, salt, Jerk Salt and bouillon powder and drizzle with the oil and 30 ml/2 tablespoons water. Toss everything together so that the vegetables are well coated with the seasonings.

Roast in the preheated oven for about 20–30 minutes until the vegetables have steamed. Remove the foil, then continue roasting for up another 30 minutes untill the veg have caramelized.

JERK JACKFRUIT SALAD

A simple salad has always been my go-to in the summer. It's quick, easy and refreshing. Bell peppers and pineapple add lashings of sweetness here, and the jackfruit adds depth and bite by giving texture. For me, this recipe has enough flavour to stand alone as a main dish, but it could also be elevated with a serving of homemade BBQ Sauce (see page 29) or Jamaican Scotch Bonnet Hot Sauce (see page 25).

2 red (bell) peppers, deseeded
   and roughly chopped
2 orange (bell) peppers, deseeded
   and roughly chopped
4 pineapple rings
1/3 bunch of fresh thyme
6 garlic cloves, crushed
1 x 400-g/14-oz. can of jackfruit,
   washed and drained
3–4 tablespoons Chef Tee's Simple
   Jerk Marinade (see page 16)
1 tablespoon caster/superfine sugar
50 ml/scant 1/4 cup olive oil

TO SERVE
Cos/romaine lettuce leaves
pumpkin seeds
grated carrot
cucumber, shaved into ribbons

SERVES 2

Preheat the oven to 220°C fan/245°C/475°F/gas 9.

Place the peppers, pineapple rings, thyme, garlic and jackfruit in a roasting tin. Add the Jerk Marinade, sugar and oil and mix to ensure all the veg is evenly coated. Add a little water to the tin as the steam will help the veg cook faster and stop the base of the tin from scorching. Cover the roasting tin tightly with foil.

Bake in the preheated oven for about 10 minutes. Remove from the oven and stir to turn all the veg over and loosen the foil so the steam can escape. Bake for another 10 minutes.

Meanwhile, prepare 2 plates (or 1 serving platter) with the salad leaves, pumpkin seeds, carrot and cucumber.

Remove the cooked veg from the tin and serve warm on the prepared salad plates.

NOTE *If you want some extra caramelization, grill/broil the jackfruit, peppers and pineapple at a high heat for a few minutes before serving.*

ITAL STEW

Interestingly all four of my grandparents had their own way of uniquely making this dish, so it only seemed right for me to come up with a recipe myself. I have simplified my dish for ease of cooking, but it can be adapted so easily with more of Mother Earth's goodness. Additions like fresh corn, chocho/chayote, carrots, spinners and sweet potato can make this dish really something extra special.

50 ml/scant ¼ cup vegetable oil
2 teaspoons dried chilli flakes/ hot pepper flakes
thumb-sized piece of fresh ginger, peeled and grated
2 teaspoons freshly ground black pepper
2 teaspoons paprika
2 teaspoons turmeric
3 tablespoons granulated sugar
1½ tablespoons good-quality vegetable bouillon or stock powder (I use vegan Marigold vegetable stock powder)
2 onions, diced
150 g/5½ oz. pumpkin or butternut squash, peeled, deseeded and diced
150 g/5½ oz. white yam, peeled and diced
200 g/7 oz. potatoes, peeled and diced
1 x 400-g/14-oz. can of red kidney beans, washed and drained
⅓ bunch of fresh thyme, sprigs snapped in half, plus extra to garnish
1 bulb of garlic, cloves separated and crushed (or 30 g/2 tablespoons garlic powder)
1 Scotch bonnet pepper, chopped for more spice or left intact for mild
½ x 400-g/14-oz can of coconut milk
wilted spinach and spinners (see page 87), to serve

SERVES 6–8

Heat the oil in a large saucepan or casserole dish, then add the dried chilli flakes, ginger, black pepper, paprika, turmeric, sugar and bouillon and mix to form a paste. Set over a low heat and add the onions, pumpkin or squash, yam and potatoes. Add 50–100 ml/scant ¼–⅓ cup water to stop the vegetables catching on the bottom of the pan.

Add the kidney beans and continue to sauté for about 15 minutes until the vegetables begin to soften, adding more water as needed. Add the thyme, garlic and Scotch bonnet and stir through.

Once the vegetables are al dente, add the coconut milk and 200–350 ml/ generous ¾–1½ cups water. Continue cooking over a low heat until the pumpkin, yams and potatoes are soft and can be broken with the light pressure of a fork against the side of the pan. Finish by stirring in extra thyme sprigs for flavour and serve with wilted spinach and spinners.

ACKEE &
BLOSSOM FRUIT

This is perhaps the most popular vegan dish that I have ever created. Ackee and saltfish is Jamaica's national dish, but thanks to some research, I found that banana blossom can be used as a great fish substitute. You will find that blossom fruit, unlike saltfish, isn't salted or dried out, so my advice is to not be afraid to be generous with the seasonings. You can also chop it up to create smaller bite-sized chunks so it absorbs the flavour better. This dish when done well is a stand-out and would do any chef proud.

40 ml/2½ tablespoons vegetable oil
1 large red or white onion, chopped
1–2 red (bell) peppers, deseeded and chopped
1 Scotch bonnet pepper, chopped
½ bunch of spring onions/scallions, chopped, white and green parts separated
1 tablespoon good-quality vegetable bouillon or stock powder (I use vegan Marigold vegetable stock powder)
1 teaspoon freshly ground black pepper
½ teaspoon icing/powdered sugar
1 x 400-g/14-oz. can of banana blossom, drained and chopped
1 x 540-g/19-oz can of ackee, drained and chopped
⅓ bunch of fresh thyme, sprigs snapped in half

TO SERVE
wilted spinach
snipped chives
Perfectly Steamed Rice
   (see page 123)

SERVES 4–6

Heat the oil in a frying pan/skillet over a medium heat and add the onion, red pepper, Scotch bonnet and white parts of the spring onion. Once the veg is slightly soft, after about 10–15 minutes, add the bouillon, black pepper and sugar. If the veg begins to stick, add a small amount of water.

Turn the heat to low and continue to sauté for a couple more minutes, so the ingredients combine to make a stock sauce, then take the pan off the heat.

Gently fold the banana blossom and ackee into the mixture in the pan. Be careful not to overmix the ackee as it is quite fragile and will break easily. Add the thyme and the green parts of the spring onions and give it a final stir together.

Serve with hot wilted spinach, chives and steamed rice.

RED PEPPER & SPINNER STEW

This recipe was created for my vegan branch and is very popular with both staff and customers. Bell peppers are a signature ingredient of mine and I think they are great for their taste and lightness. The 'spinners' are essentially boiled dumplings, which add another texture to the recipe. Together you have a dish that can be both light and filling – a perfect plant-based winter warmer.

STEW

1 kg/2¼ lb. red (bell) peppers (about 6–8), deseeded and roughly chopped

500 g/1 lb. 2 oz. onions, roughly chopped

½ bunch of fresh thyme

½ x 400-g/14-oz. can of coconut milk

10 g/2 teaspoons garlic granules

15 g/3 teaspoons freshly ground black pepper

10 g/2 teaspoons paprika

25 g/1½ tablespoons turmeric

100 g/½ cup granulated sugar

30 g/2 tablespoons good-quality vegetable bouillon or stock powder (I use vegan Marigold vegetable stock powder)

25 ml/1½ tablespoons vegetable oil

wilted spinach and snipped chives, to serve

SPINNERS

300 g/2¼ cups plain/all-purpose flour, plus extra for dusting

1 tablespoon caster/superfine sugar

pinch of table salt

15 ml/1 tablespoon vegetable oil

50 ml/3½ tablespoons plant-based milk

SERVES 6–8

Place all the ingredients for the stew, except the spinach and chives, in a large saucepan with 500 ml/2 cups water and set over a high heat. Bring to the boil, then turn down the heat slightly and simmer for about 40–60 minutes until the vegetables have sweated down and softened.

Meanwhile, make the dumpling mixture. Place the flour, sugar and salt in a large bowl. Put the oil, milk and 150 ml/⅔ cup water in a jug/pitcher and mix together. Slowly pour the liquid mixture into the flour, little by little, and mix and knead until the mixture is sticky and has come together into a dough.

Dust your hands with flour, then pull out a piece of the dough, roughly the size of your palm, and gently roll it into a small cylinder shape. Repeat this until the mixture is used up.

Place the dumplings in the stew and stir them in once all added. Cover the pan with a lid and continue cooking the stew and dumplings for another 10–15 minutes until the spinners are cooked all the way through (they should be slightly chewy). Serve the stew with some wilted spinach and snipped chives if liked.

NOTE *You could use a full tin of coconut milk in this recipe. However, bear in mind that this will shorten the shelf-life of the stew and it will then need to be consumed within 24 hours.*

TRINIDADIAN BUS UP SHUT ROTI

Roti is a staple in the Caribbean and varied types can be found across the islands. In Paradise Cove, we use dal puri roti, which is made from wheat flour and chickpeas. We make wraps and serve it with stews, but bus up shut is equally delicious and I find it works better with curries.

Now, bus up shut is said to resemble a 'busted up t-shirt' and is comparable to paratha in its texture. The key is to not skimp on the butter to be able to achieve lamination – this gives the flaky texture that so many crave.

This recipe is a hard one to crack, so go slow, follow the steps and enjoy!

600 g/4½ cups plain/all-purpose flour, plus extra for dusting
1–2 tablespoons baking powder
generous pinch of table salt
1 teaspoon ground cinnamon (optional)
2–3 tablespoons caster/superfine sugar, to taste
200–250 ml/generous ¾–1 cup oat milk, at room temperature
200–400 g/generous ¾–1¾ cups plant-based unsalted butter, at room temperature (see Note opposite)

MAKES 6–8 ROTI

Sieve the flour into a mixing bowl and add the baking powder, salt, cinnamon, if using, and sugar.

Combine the oat milk with 200 ml/generous ¾ cup water in a jug/pitcher. Slowly add the liquid to the flour mixture, combining to create a dough; stop adding liquid once the dough is smooth and soft and able to hold a ball shape.

Rub the dough ball generously with some of the butter, coating it all over, then cover the bowl with a clean dish towel. Set aside to rest for 15–20 minutes.

Sprinkle the work surface with flour. Cut the dough ball into 6–8 equal pieces, forming them into smaller balls. Rub these smaller dough balls generously with butter, coating them all over, then cover with a dish towel and set aside to rest for 10 minutes.

Sprinkle the work surface with flour again, and use a rolling pin to roll one of the dough balls into a 26-cm/10¼-in. circle, about 5 mm/⅛ in. thick. Cover the rolled out dough circle in a generous layer of butter. Cut a slit from the centre point of the dough circle to the edge (see left), then roll your dough around from one cut edge to another, to make a cone shape.

Take the wide end of the cone and press the edges in towards the middle, sealing the shape and flattening your cone. Do the same with the opposite end of the cone, pressing down the point to form a flattened dumpling shape. Repeat with the remaining balls. Let them rest, covered, for 20 minutes.

Heat a large flat-bed frying pan/skillet, griddle/ridged stove-top grill pan (or traditionally a tawah) over a high heat.

Roll out each dough ball on a floured surface into a 26-cm/10¼-in. circle, making sure it is even in thickness all over. Coat the surface of the hot pan generously with butter, then immediately place the dough circle on the hot pan and coat it with more butter as it cooks – this should take about 1 minute. Use 2 spatulas to flip the roti over and cook for another minute.

At this point the roti should now be evenly cooked on both sides and slightly golden. Use both spatulas to crumple the roti from the outer edges inwards, to scrunch it up, then flip again, doing this a couple of times until it is flaky and golden all the way through. Set aside on a plate and repeat with the remaining balls of dough.

Serve with Pumpkin Curry (see opposite).

NOTES

★ *The amount of butter used depends on your preferences, using more butter will result in more lamination and a really delicious flaky texture.*

★ *This recipe also works well with dairy milk and butter, so feel free to use these instead if you are not vegan.*

PUMPKIN CURRY

30 ml/2 tablespoons vegetable oil
600 g/1 lb. 5 oz. pumpkin, peeled, deseeded and cut into chunks
1 chocho/chayote, peeled and roughly chopped
2 onions, roughly chopped
1 Scotch bonnet pepper, chopped
⅓ bunch of fresh thyme
thumb-sized piece of fresh ginger, peeled and grated
1 teaspoon garlic powder (see Note below)
1 teaspoon pimento berries
1 tablespoon good-quality vegetable bouillon or stock (I use vegan Marigold vegetable stock powder)
½ teaspoon turmeric
½ teaspoon ground cumin
½ teaspoon paprika
1½ teaspoons caster/superfine sugar
Bus Up Shut Roti (see opposite), to serve

SERVES 4–6

Heat the oil in a large saucepan over a medium heat. Add the pumpkin, chocho, onions, Scotch bonnet peppers, thyme and ginger and cook for 5 minutes until the vegetables start to colour. Add the garlic powder, pimento berries and bouillon and mix to a paste, ensuring the vegetables are browned in the oil and seasoning. If it scorches, add a little water.

Add the turmeric, cumin, paprika, sugar and 200 ml/generous ¾ cup water to the pan and simmer for about 30 minutes until thickened and the pumpkin is soft. Taste to check the seasoning and add a little more bouillon, ½ teaspoon at a time, if needed. Serve with the Bus Up Shut Roti.

NOTE *For best results use garlic powder, not granules or salt. If garlic powder isn't available, try using freshly grated or crushed garlic instead.*

SWEET POTATO & SWEETCORN CAKES

I've always had a recipe for pumpkin and crab cakes, but it got me thinking how I could make some plant-based savoury patties incorporating sweet potato. After a few trials I finally managed this delicious recipe. The trick is to make sure your sweet potatoes are dried out once cooked, as this creates a better texture. These cakes are pretty versatile and are delicious on their own, with a dip or could even be a burger!

4 large orange sweet potatoes
2 spring onions/scallions, chopped
1 teaspoon paprika
½ teaspoon dried chilli flakes/ hot pepper flakes
1 teaspoon garlic powder (see page 187)
a pinch of sea salt
5 heaped tablespoons oat flour
½ x 340-g/12-oz can of sweetcorn, drained
olive oil, for frying
balsamic glaze, to serve (optional)

MAKES 6 LARGE OR 12 SMALL CAKES

Preheat the oven to 220°C fan/245°C/475°F/gas 9. Line a baking tray with non-stick baking paper.

Pierce the sweet potatoes all over with a fork and wrap them individually in foil. Roast in the preheated oven for 30–40 minutes until soft. Alternatively, pierce the potatoes and microwave them for about 10–15 minutes until soft.

Remove the cooked potatoes from the oven or microwave (leaving the oven on if you used the oven) and slice them open. Use a spoon to scrape out the potato flesh into a bowl and use a potato masher or fork to mash the potato. The potatoes should be rather dry in texture. If they seem wet – which means not enough moisture has evaporated during cooking – place the scooped out potato flesh back in the microwave for an extra 10 minutes or back in the oven for another 20 minutes.

Add the remaining ingredients, except the olive oil and balsamic glaze, to the bowl with the mashed sweet potato and use a fork to mix everything together. Form palm-sized portions of the mixture into small patties, about 4–6 cm/10–15 in. in diameter and 1 cm/½ in. thick.

Reduce or set the oven temperature to 160°C fan/180°C/350°F/gas 4. Place the patties on the lined baking tray and bake in the preheated oven for 20–30 minutes until they are starting to turn golden.

For an extra crisp finish, heat a little olive oil in a frying pan/skillet over a medium heat and cook the patties for 2–4 minutes on each side until golden brown or slightly charred.

Drizzle with a balsamic glaze if liked and serve with a simple salad, curry or fish dish of your choosing.

PLANTAIN BURGERS WITH GRILLED PEPPERS

There are so many Black chefs in the UK who have created their own brands and eateries and this recipe was inspired by them. We're all unique in our heritage and style, but a love of plantain seems to be the one thing we all have in common, so how could I not include the famous plantain burger? With this recipe I have added my own touch by including my jerk salt, which complements the plantain well. I have discovered that ripe plantain will need less seasoning than under-ripe plantain so start off with 1 tablespoon, and add more if needed.

1 x 400-g/14-oz can of black beans, washed and drained
1 large ripe (but not overripe) plantain, peeled, topped and tailed
1–2 tablespoons Brixton-inspired Jerk Salt (see page 26), depending on the ripeness of the plantain
1 teaspoon olive oil, plus extra for frying
½ carrot, peeled and grated
1 red (bell) pepper, deseeded and chopped (half for grilling and half for the burger)
2 tablespoons plain/all-purpose flour
1 tablespoon caster/superfine sugar, plus extra for grilling the peppers

TO SERVE
4 vegan brioche buns
salad leaves
vegan mayonaise
sliced red onion
cucumber ribbons

SERVES 4

Preheat the oven to 160°C fan/180°C/350°F/gas 4.

Put the black beans and plantain in a bowl with the Jerk Salt, olive oil, grated carrot and half the red pepper. Mash together, being careful not to overwork as leaving some chunkier beans will make a nicer texture. Add the flour and sugar and mix together until combined.

Shape the mixture into 4 patties and wrap them in some baking paper or cling film/plastic wrap and chill for at least 10 minutes.

Warm a griddle pan/ridged stove-top grill pan over a high heat with a little olive oil. Add the remaining chopped red pepper and cook for a minute or two with a little sugar until it starts to caramelize. Remove the peppers from the pan and set aside.

Add the burgers to the pan with a little more oil and sear them over a high heat on both sides so that the surface caramelizes, then turn the heat to low and cook for a few minutes until the burgers are piping hot inside.

Serve the burgers in vegan brioche buns with the grilled red pepper, salad leaves, vegan mayonnaise, sliced red onion and cucumber ribbons if liked.

NOTE *You could use oats instead of flour – this will add a denser texture to the burgers.*

HOMEMADE BEAN BURGERS

This recipe goes way back to the days when I was cooking from home. Initially, when trialling my recipe I found it hard to get the right balance of beans, as I was only using one type. But I then realized that mixed beans give not only different textures, but grill brilliantly too.

1 x 400-g/14-oz. can of mixed peas and beans
1 teaspoon olive oil, plus extra for frying the burgers
½ carrot, peeled and grated
2–4 garlic cloves, crushed
¼ onion, finely chopped
1 tablespoon Chef Tee's Simple Jerk Marinade (see page 16)
2 tablespoons plain/all-purpose flour
1 teaspoon caster/superfine sugar

TO SERVE
vegan brioche buns
grilled pineapple rings
spinach
vegan mayonnaise
sliced red onion
plantain wedges

SERVES 4–6

Preheat the oven to 160°C fan/180°C/350°F/gas 4.

Wash and drain the peas and beans, then mash them in a bowl. Do not over mash, as leaving some whole beans helps to give a nicer texture. Set aside.

Heat the olive oil in a frying pan/skillet, then add the carrot and cook over a gentle heat for about 2 minutes. Add the garlic, onion and Jerk Marinade and cook for 1–2 minutes until the carrot and onions have softened slightly. Set aside to cool.

Add the cooled vegetable mixture to the mashed beans along with the flour and sugar and mix until combined. Shape the mixture into 4–6 patties and wrap them in some baking paper or cling film/plastic wrap and chill for at least 10 minutes.

When you are ready to cook, warm a frying pan/skillet or griddle/ridged stove-top grill pan with a little olive oil. Sear/caramelize the burgers on both sides over a high heat to get some colour on them, then turn the heat to low to warm the patties through for a few minutes more. Try not to cook the burgers for more than 10 minutes in total, otherwise they will dry out.

Serve the bean burgers in vegan brioche buns with grilled pineapple rings, spinach, vegan mayonnaise, sliced red onion and perhaps some plantain wedges on the side.

NOTE *You could use oats instead of flour – this will add a denser texture to the burgers.*

CARIBBEAN CLASSICS & MAINS

MEAT & POULTRY DISHES

Welcome to the heart of this book, where you will find recipes for the staples of the Caribbean islands. I am often asked what my favourite thing to eat is… and I confess it is fried dumplings. But when asked what my favourite dish is to cook, I immediately think of my curried goat and jerk chicken and the other recipes found in this chapter.

These recipes are utterly just my pride and joy – they took years of practice to get right, but I know them all by heart and I can cook them all with my eyes closed. They produce powerful memories for me, as each recipe was self-taught and practiced again until I found the perfect combination of flavours.

This isn't a chapter to rush, and some recipes require more time, but, like me, try to enjoy every minute of it, as the result will be something really special.

Above left: Coffee Plantation, Blue Mountains, Saint Thomas Parish, Jamaica. Above right: Scotch bonnet peppers growing in the sunshine.

CLASSIC CURRIED GOAT

I was taught how to make this dish by a chef I used to work with in Brixton. Janine taught me to wash the meat thoroughly and the importance of using a good, strong curry powder. Goat/mutton is an 'old' meat and therefore requires long cooking times. When cooking it in a cast-iron casserole dish, it requires numerous refills of water to stop the pot burning as the water evaporates during the long cooking time, which can be anything from 2–6 hours. Like most of my dishes, I believe the key to success here is creating a good stock, as that's where all the flavours come from. Just remember to keep adding water and only remove the lid to intentionally reduce the liquid – or as Janine told me, 'to burn it off' – once the meat is cooked and soft.

500 g–1 kg/1 lb. 2 oz.–2¼ lb.
   boneless goat leg, chopped into
   chunks, washed and patted dry
40 ml/2½ tablespoons vegetable oil
2 tablespoons good-quality
   vegetable bouillon or stock
   powder (I use Marigold vegetable
   stock powder)
1 tablespoon curry powder
   (for best results use Betapac
   Jamaican curry powder)
15 g/1 tablespoon turmeric
15 g/1 tablespoon paprika
5 g/1 teaspoon pimento berries
pinch of mixed spice
5 g/1 teaspoon ground cumin
2–3 large onions, rouchly chopped
1 bunch of spring onions/scallions,
   roughly chopped
thumb-sized piece of fresh ginger,
   peeled and grated
1 bulb of garlic, cloves separated
   and chopped
2 Scotch bonnet peppers, roughly
   chopped (or 1 for a milder heat)
200 g/7 oz. Maris Piper potatoes,
   peeled and diced
½ bunch of fresh thyme, sprigs
   snapped in half

SERVES 8–12

Place the meat, oil, bouillon, curry powder, turmeric, paprika, pimento berries, mixed spice and cumin in a cast-iron casserole dish/Dutch oven set over a high heat. Cook, stirring to seal in the seasoning, for a couple of minutes until the meat has browned all over.

Add enough water to the pot to completely cover the meat, then add the onions, spring onions, ginger, garlic and Scotch bonnets and stir to combine. Bring to the boil, cover the pot with a lid and continue to cook at a rolling boil over a high heat with the lid on for 2–3 hours. Check every 20–30 minutes to see how tender the meat is and top up the water as needed, as it will evaporate during the long cooking process.

After about 2–3 hours the meat should be soft, however this varies greatly depending on the cut of meat. If it's not soft yet, continue to cook at a rolling boil until it is. Once the meat is tender, it should be able to be split with a fork against the side of the dish with minimal pressure. Remove the lid and continue to cook, allowing any excess water to evaporate. Once the water has reduced to be level with the meat, add the potatoes and cook for 20–30 minutes until the potatoes are soft.

Remove from the heat and stir in the thyme for an aromatic flavour or garnish with sprigs for a lighter hint of thyme. Serve hot with the rice or roti of your choice.

NOTE *It is unlikely but possible to overcook goat, which will result in more of a pulled meat stew. For example, if you decide to use a pressure cooker the steam will cook the meat much faster than water. Therefore, I would always suggest learning the old-fashioned way first.*

CLASSIC CURRIED CHICKEN

My curried chicken is an easy dish. I think I was 18 when I first came up with this recipe. In fact, if I looked hard enough, I could probably find the waiters notepad that it was written on. Like my curried goat, the secret is to create a good stock, as this is where the deep curry flavour comes from. I also always try to use organic or better quality produce, as you find it doesn't skimp on flavour.

Unlike goat, chicken is a white meat and becomes tender fairly quickly, so care must be taken not to add too much water to the pot or cook the meat for too long when trying to reduce the sauce. Finally, try substituting the chicken for vegetables to make a delicious plant-based curry.

500 g–1 kg/1 lb. 2 oz.–2¼ lb. chicken breast or thigh, diced

40 ml/2½ tablespoons vegetable oil

2 tablespoons good-quality vegetable bouillon or stock powder (I use Marigold vegetable stock powder)

1 tablespoon curry powder (for best results use Betapac Jamaican curry powder)

10 g/2 teaspoons turmeric

10 g/2 teaspoons paprika

5 g/1 teaspoon pimento berries

pinch of mixed spice

pinch of ground cumin

1 large onion, roughly chopped

1 bunch of spring onions/scallions, roughly chopped

thumb-sized piece of fresh ginger, peeled and grated

½ bulb of garlic, cloves peeled and crushed

1 Scotch bonnet pepper, roughly chopped

200 g/7 oz. Maris Piper potatoes, peeled and diced

½ bunch of fresh thyme, sprigs snapped in half

SERVES 8–12

Place the chicken, oil, bouillon, curry powder, turmeric, paprika, pimento berries, mixed spice and cumin in a cast-iron casserole dish/Dutch oven set over a high heat. Cook, stirring the meat to seal in the seasoning, for a few minutes until the chicken has turned white all over.

Add enough water to just about cover the meat, then add the onion, spring onions, ginger, garlic and Scotch bonnet pepper and stir to combine. Bring to the boil, cover the pot with a lid and continue to cook at a rolling boil over a high heat with the lid on for 20–30 minutes. Do not add any further water as this would wash the flavour away and risk overcooking the meat.

Once the chicken is white all the way through, remove the lid and add the potatoes. Continue to cook for a final 30 minutes until the potatoes are soft. To help remove any excess liquid, keep the lid off to speed up reduction.

Once cooked, remove from the heat and stir in the thyme sprigs for an aromatic flavour or garnish with sprigs for a lighter hint of thyme. Serve hot with the rice or roti of your choice.

OVEN-BAKED JERK CHICKEN

I personally don't like the smoky taste of a barbecue. I have also grown up in central London where not everyone has a garden, so a lot of my recipes are made for those with similar set-ups. What I would say about this dish, is it is so important to get your marinade right. My personal preference is for organic, free-range, no MSG enhanced flavourings, hence why I have always been adamant about making my own jerk. A good strong marinade is key, but you will also want something for colour. I have chosen dark soy sauce, which mimics Jamaican 'browning' and acts as flavour enhancer. It also stops the base of the roasting tin scorching.

4–6 skin-on, bone-in chicken leg pieces, (see Note below)
2–3 tablespoons Chef Tee's Simple Jerk Marinade (see page 16) per chicken leg
100 ml/generous ⅓ cup strong dark soy sauce

SERVES 4–6

Preheat the oven to 220°C fan/245°C/475°F/gas 9. Prepare the chicken by removing any fat, sinew or chicken hairs (use the sharpest part of a knife to scrape the chicken skin, removing any unwanted hairs).

Rub the Jerk Marinade vigorously into the chicken legs, pushing the marinade under the skin so it is all well coated. Place the chicken pieces in a roasting tin.

Mix the soy sauce with 200 ml/generous ¾ cup water in a jug/pitcher, then pour it into the tin around the chicken (not over it), until the liquid comes to just halfway up the chicken legs.

Roast the chicken on the top shelf of the preheated oven for 1 hour. The chicken will be cooked after 40 minutes or so, but keep roasting to give the signature barbecue colour.

NOTES

★ You can use chicken breasts instead of leg pieces if you prefer, but you will need to cover the roasting tin with foil and cook for only 30 minutes, as chicken breasts often dry out quickly.

★ If you're unsure whether the chicken is cooked, the skin should have pulled away from the leg bone, exposing it, if it is.

★ If you love crispy chicken skin, use a griddle or frying pan/skillet, with a little oil set over a high heat to sear the chicken before serving.

SIMPLE JERK PORK RIBS

One of my earliest recipes was these pork ribs. I taught myself by watching the chefs at work and using online recipes when I was about 18. One of the chefs I worked with, Bob, was rarely miserable... but when he was we would all know about it! On his better days, he would frequently pull me aside to impart a golden nugget of cooking advice: 'T, you ave fi rub di ribs' ('You have to rub the ribs'). At this point Bob was no longer facing me and arduously massaging his ribs with marinade. He then turned his face to me and chuckled as he added the water to the sides of the tray... 'this stops it scorching'.

I didn't really understand why he was chuckling until I did things for myself, but adding the little water helped cook the ribs in a steam, not a dry heat, meaning they cooked faster and without burning. Bob, you're a genius.

500 g/1 lb. 2 oz. pork spare ribs, trimmed to 4 cm/1½ in. long (you can ask your butcher to do this for you)
150 g/5½ oz. Chef Tee's Simple Jerk Marinade (see page 16)
120 ml/½ cup soy sauce

SERVES 6–8

Preheat the oven to 220°C fan/245°C/475°F/gas 9.

Place the spare ribs in a roasting tin. Rub the Jerk Marinade vigorously all over the meat, making sure it is well coated.

Mix the soy sauce with 100 ml/generous ⅓ cup water in a jug/pitcher or cup, then pour it around the ribs, not over them.

Cover the roasting tin tightly with foil and roast in the preheated oven for 2 hours, or until the rib meat is tender. If the ribs are not tender at this point, continue to cook for a little longer, checking at 20-minute intervals.

Once cooked, remove from the oven and serve as desired.

CLASSIC STEWED CHICKEN

*Stew chicken is one of my newer recipes, however it's one that I find isn't popular.
In St Lucia and Jamaica, I found curried chicken to be the most popular dish among
street vendors, and in my restaurant the bestseller has always been Classic Curried
Goat (see page 102). For me, stewed chicken is an under-rated, knockout dish, which
takes me right back to cooking with my godmother, at her house – just the two of us
– at a really peaceful time when she was still looking after me. I was about 12 and in
her house in Thornton Heath. She would be cooking so effortlessly... just throwing
in some seasonings left, right and centre, then it was done. The perfect stew chicken!
With added fresh spinach to just lift the dish – this dish is utter heaven for me.*

500 g–1 kg/1 lb. 2 oz.–2¼ lb. skinless,
   boneless chicken breast or thigh,
   diced
40 ml/2½ tablespoons vegetable oil
2 tablespoons good-quality
   vegetable bouillon or stock
   powder (I use Marigold vegetable
   stock powder)
20 g/¾ oz. turmeric
5 g/1 teaspoon pimento berries
15 g/1 tablespoon granulated sugar
15 g/1 tablespoon garlic granules
pinch of ground allspice
5 g/1 teaspoon ground cumin
200 g/7 oz. onions, roughly chopped
thumb-sized piece of ginger, peeled
   and grated
½ bulb of garlic, cloves chopped
1 Scotch bonnet pepper, diced
½ bunch of fresh thyme, sprigs
   snapped in half
1 bunch of spring onions/scallions,
   roughly chopped
2 handfuls of baby spinach leaves

SERVES 6–10

Place the meat, oil, bouillon, turmeric, pimento berries, sugar, garlic granules, mixed spice and cumin in a cast-iron casserole dish/Dutch oven set over a high heat. Cook, stirring to seal in the seasoning, for a few minutes until the meat has turned white all over.

Add enough water to just about cover the meat, then add the onions, ginger, garlic and Scotch bonnet pepper and stir to combine. Bring to the boil, cover the pot with a lid and continue to cook at a rolling boil over a high heat for 20–30 minutes. Do not add any further water as this will wash the flavour away and risk overcooking the meat.

Once the chicken is white all the way through, remove the lid and continue to cook for a final 10 minutes until any excess liquid has reduced and the sauce has thickened.

Remove from the heat and stir in the thyme, spring onions and add spinach leaves to wilt.

NOTE *Typically stewed chicken is cooked with browning to create 'brown stew chicken', which this dish resembles. To give it its distinctive brown colour, add 2 tablespoons Jamaican browning or dark soy sauce when sealing the meat.*

OXTAIL STEW WITH BUTTER BEANS & CARROTS

People always ask what is my favourite dish, and I rarely ever know. But, I know oxtail stew is one of the dishes that I like a lot. Oxtail, like goat, is a cheap cut of meat, so takes a long time to cook, but when done properly, it is sensational.

It can be an exceptionally fatty meat, so care should be taken to skim off the fat once cooked, otherwise you will have a layer of oil that isn't palatable. Carrots are optional but generally speaking, white butter beans are a must. They soak up the flavour and add to the layers of texture.

500 g–1 kg/1 lb. 2 oz.–2¼ lb oxtail, chopped into halves

120ml/½ cup dark soy sauce

1 teaspoon pimento berries

1 tablespoon good-quality vegetable bouillon or stock powder (I use Marigold vegetable stock powder), plus extra if needed

1 teaspoon freshly ground black pepper

½ bulb of garlic, cloves separated and peeled

2 large onions, quartered

10 g/½ oz. fresh thyme, sprigs snapped in half

thumb-sized piece of fresh ginger, peeled

1 Scotch bonnet pepper

1 carrot, peeled and chopped

1 x 400-g/14-oz. can of butter beans, rinsed and drained

TO FINISH

1 bunch of spring onions/scallions, chopped

½ bunch fresh thyme, sprigs snapped in half

SERVES 6–10

Place the oxtail halves in a cast-iron casserole dish/Dutch oven and add the soy sauce, pimento berries, bouillon and black pepper and use your hands to rub this all over the oxtail so it is well coated.

Put the garlic, onions, thyme, ginger and Scotch bonnet pepper in a food processor and pulse into a paste. Add this to the casserole dish along with 1 litre/4 cups water.

Set the casserole dish over a high heat, bring to the boil, then cover the pot with a lid and continue to cook at a rolling boil for about 2–3 hours. Check every 30 minutes on the tenderness of the oxtail and top up the water as needed, as it will evaporate during the long cooking process.

After anywhere between 2–3 hours the oxtail should be soft. If it's not, continue to cook at a rolling boil until it is. Once the meat is tender and able to be easily split with a fork against the side of the dish, remove the lid, add the carrot and butter beans and continue to cook over a high heat for a final 30 minutes until the carrots have softened and any excess liquid has reduced. Taste for seasoning and add another tablespoon of bouillon if needed.

Once the carrots are cooked and the liquid has reduced to a saucey consistency, remove the stew from the heat and stir in the spring onions and snapped thyme sprigs before serving.

JERK BURGERS

Working at a barbecue/grill smokehouse in Clapham taught me a lot. I saw so many ways to cook meats, then one day I thought about combining them with my marinade. The restaurant I worked at had a special sausage and burger made with their spices and I thought I would try something similar. Clapham has many well-known butchers and I slowly began asking them for advice on how to make a jerk burger. Through trial and error, I discovered the key was all in the marinade. A poorly made marinade gives poor results, and therefore we will save the story of me crunching pimento seeds in my burger for another day!

I find that this burger is best served medium-well–well, as you want to make sure the jerk marinade is well cooked through.

300–500 g/10½ oz.–1 lb. 2 oz. minced/ground beef
3–4 teaspoons Chef Tee's Simple Jerk Marinade (see page 16)
4 teaspoons dark soy sauce
vegetable oil, for frying

TO SERVE
floured buns
salad leaves
mayonnaise
sliced red onion
sliced tomatoes

MAKES ABOUT 3–5 BURGERS

Place the meat in a bowl and gently pat in the marinade. Add the soy sauce and gently mix through.

Take about 100 g/3½ oz. of meat at a time, and form into burger patty shapes using your hands.

Heat a little oil in a frying pan/skillet over a medium heat and fry the burgers until they are evenly coloured on both sides, taking care to ensure the sides are cooked also. For a medium burger, aim for 5–6 minutes cooking time and 10–12 minutes for a well-done burger.

Once cooked to your desired rareness, leave to rest in the pan for 2 minutes, then serve in buns with salad leaves, mayo, sliced red onion and tomato, or as liked.

Should you have any spare burgers, wrap these in baking paper before cooking and keep refrigerated for up to 3 days.

SIDE DISHES

THE PERFECT ACCOMPANIMENT TO COMPLETE ANY CARIBBEAN MEAL

We say in the Caribbean that 'a guest must leave the house with a smile on their face because their belly is full'. And there is only one way to do that – by accompanying the main meal with a selection of delicious sides.

Every island has their 'own' way of doing things, but what is fascinating is that our classic sides have evolved with the new generation of Black British cuisine. There is simply no right or wrong way to do it, as long as you cook with your heart. Food moves with the times. You see, we're more conscious as a society and other cultures continue to influence us.

So, here you can find some classics that you would see all over the Caribbean, as well as some recipes with modern-inspired influences to accompany your main dishes.

Above left: Fruit shops and fruit selling
on the roads of the Dominican Republic.
Above right: Jamaica yellow door keyhole.

ROASTED PEPPER & PINEAPPLE SALAD WITH LIME

I adore this salad. It's simple, quick and easily adaptable. The secret here is to use my classic homemade jerk marinade (see page 16) but you could also use the plant-based marinade (see page 22). What is great is that a salad like this has a mixture of sharpness from the spices and sweetness from the pineapple, creating a balance of flavours.

Should you wish to jazz this up further, add some roasted goats' cheese and roasted tomatoes. Heaven!

splash of vegetable oil, for frying
2 red (bell) peppers, deseeded and
   roughly chopped into chunks
½ pineapple, peeled, cored and
   roughly chopped into chunks
2 tablespoons Chef Tee's Simple Jerk
   Marinade (see page 16)
½ bunch of fresh thyme, sprigs
   snapped in half

TO SERVE
salad leaves
juice of ½ lime

SERVES 4–6

Heat the oil in a frying pan/skillet over a high heat and add the red peppers and pineapple. Add the Jerk Marinade and thyme sprigs and stir to mix. Cook for about 5–10 minutes, stirring continuously, until the peppers are soft. If the peppers begin to stick, add a small amount of water. Remove the pan from the heat and leave to cool.

Prepare the salad leaves on a serving platter and top with the cooked pineapple and red peppers.

Drizzle over the juices from the frying pan and finish by squeezing over the lime juice.

PERFECTLY STEAMED RICE

'T, even di best chef dem, dem ah ago spoil rice'…
What does this mean? I asked a chef when she told
me this – it's simply an old Jamaican expression
meaning that even the best chefs spoil rice.

So many of us cheat and now with microwave
rice available, cooking rice is a skill that is sadly
being lost with time. I was first taught by my uncle
to merely add rice to the pan, then cover it with
a fingertips worth of water. My best friend's mum
taught me to simply just boil it and drain off the
excess water. Both work, but only if Lady Luck is
on your side.

The point is, cooking rice is hard and it's a skill.
It wasn't until I opened my restaurant, even after
years of cooking it, that I worked out the perfect
ratio of rice to water.

So here it is – just follow this ratio and no
matter what, your rice will be perfectly steamed.

50 ml/3½ tablespoons vegetable oil
1 teaspoon sea salt
900 g/2 lb. basmati rice

SERVES 6–12

Add all the ingredients to a large saucepan with
1.35 litres/5¾ cups water and bring to the boil.
Turn the heat to the lowest possible setting, then
carefully cover the pan with foil and place the lid on
top. Steam for 10–15 minutes until the rice is fluffy
and tender and all the water has been absorbed.

NOTES
If you are cooking for less people, use the following
ratios (with the same amount of oil and salt as above):

★ *For 1–2 people – use 225 g/8 oz. rice and 375 ml/*
scant 1²/3 cups water.

★ *For 2–4 people – use 450 g/1 lb. rice and 750 ml/*
3¼ cups water.

COLESLAW

Nothing beats a well-made coleslaw. And you know the one I mean... the one that is made at Christmas and then eaten with dinner. And then eaten at night when you're carefully sneaking around and picking at the food in the fridge. And then eaten again the next day with Christmas leftovers and cheese in a sandwich. Ohh yes, that kind of coleslaw is something most Black British households know about!

The trick is to sweeten your coleslaw with sugar, agave or syrup – something that dissolves easily – and to not make it with too much mayonnaise, as the vegetables release water. Everyone who visits Paradise Cove asks us for our coleslaw recipe, so I hope our loyal fans enjoy.

300 g/10½ oz. carrots, peeled
  and grated
150 g/5½ oz. Savoy cabbage,
  core removed and thinly sliced
  or shredded
1 red onion, thinly sliced
2 tablespoons icing/powdered sugar
grated zest of ½ lemon
150 g/²/3 cup mayonnaise (or add
  more for a creamier coleslaw)
100 g/1 packed cup grated
  Cheddar cheese (optional)

SERVES 4–6

Place the carrots, cabbage and onion in a large mixing bowl. Add the remaining ingredients and cheese, if using, and mix until well combined.

NOTES

★ *All the vegetables can be shredded in a food processor using the slicing and grating blade to save time.*

★ *The leaves of a Savoy cabbage are best for coleslaw, in colour and texture.*

★ *Grated lemon zest works better than lemon juice, as this can split the mayonnaise. You could use lemon juice if you are planning on eating the coleslaw the same day it is made though.*

CLASSIC RICE & PEAS

I have watched adults cook this dish all my life and I couldn't cook it myself until I was about 18! I recall standing at work in Brixton, attempting to cook rice and peas, ambitiously choosing the biggest pot in the restaurant to use. A few moments later I was then laughing with the owner and prep chef because I had added too much water to the pot. In his Jamaican voice, Johnson the prep chef explained 'It will turn to mud', and he stepped in, drained off some excess water and placed a slice of bread on top of the pot, saving the rice and peas. Everyone has their way of cooking rice and peas. Differences include basmati rice or easy-cook rice, kidney beans or gungo peas, white or red onions, it is really down to personal preference. However, my tastebuds prefer this version made with basmati, red peas and onions.

450 g/2²/₃ cups basmati rice
40 ml/2½ tablespoons vegetable oil
1½ red onions, diced
2 spring onions/scallions, diced
1 teaspoon sea salt
1½ teaspoons good-quality
    vegetable bouillon or stock
    powder (I use Marigold vegetable
    stock powder)
1 x 400-g/14-oz. can of peas (gungo
    or black-eye peas or kidney beans),
    washed and drained
½ x 400-g/14-oz. can of coconut
    milk
½ bunch of fresh thyme, sprigs
    snapped in half

SERVES 6–12

Wash the rice in a bowl of water, then rinse and drain. Do this three times to remove any dirt and take away the starch from the rice. Set aside.

Heat the oil in a large saucepan over a high heat and add the onions, spring onions, salt, bouillon, peas, coconut milk, thyme and 800 ml/3¹/₃ cups water. Bring to the boil and cook for 10–15 minutes until the onions have softened and all the ingredients have been infused by the coconut milk.

Add the rice, stir to combine with the other ingredients and reduce the heat to the lowest possible setting. Cover the pan with foil, add the lid and let the rice steam for 30–40 minutes, stirring only once or twice throughout cooking to ensure the peas and onions mix thoroughly into the rice. Once the rice has cooked, remove the lid and foil and serve.

NOTES

★ *If you have added too much water, remove the lid to let the excess liquid evaporate. Place a slice of bread on top of the rice as this will absorb the excess water.*

★ *If you have not added enough water, add 100 ml/¹/₃ cup more water, seal the top of the pan with foil and the lid again and cook until the rice is cooked.*

★ *It is normal for the bottom of the pot to burn slightly – this is traditionally called 'pot bottom' in the Caribbean. If you have 'pot bottom', you have cooked the rice and peas correctly.*

★ *If you're using dried kidney beans or peas instead of canned, you will need to soak them overnight, then boil them until soft before using in this dish. They have to be soft or else you risk food poisoning from the lectin. Once boiled, they provide the best colouring for a classic rice and peas dish.*

KALE, CABBAGE & CALLALOO

Callaloo is what I would call Jamaican spinach. It's bursting with iron, wilts down wonderfully and tastes great. I created this dish in tribute to one 'ole lickle Jamican lady' I once upon a time knew, called Miss India. She was one of the best chefs I knew, and her callaloo was one of a kind. She taught me to sauté and how to balance seasonings and, without her, I wouldn't have thought to season or add other flavourings.

50 ml/3½ tablespoons vegetable oil
1 red (bell) pepper, chopped
1–2 onions (about 200 g/7 oz.), chopped
200 g/7 oz. kale, woody stems removed
1 Savoy cabbage, core removed and
   leaves chopped
½ bunch of fresh thyme, sprigs
   snapped in half
1 x 400-g/14-oz. can of callaloo, drained
1 tablespoon good-quality vegetable
   bouillon or stock powder (I use
   Marigold vegetable stock powder)
½ tablespoon ground black pepper

SERVES 6–8

Heat the oil in a large pan set over a high heat and sauté the red pepper, onions, kale and cabbage. Add the thyme, and if the veg begins to stick on the base of the pan, add a little water to help it move along.

Add the callaloo to the pan and continue to sauté until the vegetables begin to soften; this should take between 10–15 minutes in total. Often the chunkier the veg, the longer it will take to sauté.

Lower the heat to medium and add the bouillon and black pepper. Continue to sauté for 2–3 minutes for the ingredients to combine into a stock/sauce. Leave to cool or serve hot.

SIMPLE SAUTÉED VEG

Things like sautéed veg with cabbage and peppers all form part of an ital diet in the Caribbean. Ital food was one of the original forms of the more commonly stylized 'plant-based diet'. However, unlike today's plant-based offerings, ital food tends to remain more in its natural state, and doesn't attempt to recreate meat flavours or textures. With this dish, I have chosen not only vegetables that I love, but ones that have a variety of texture and colour and retain water, creating a lovely juice when seasoned.

1 red (bell) pepper, deseeded
   and chopped into chunky slices
1 Savoy cabbage, core removed
   and leaves thinly sliced
1 carrot, peeled and grated
1 red onion, thinly sliced
1 chocho/chayote, core removed
   and chopped into chunks
handful of okra (about 5–10),
   topped and tailed
½ teaspoon good-quality vegetable
   bouillon or stock powder (I use
   Marigold vegetable stock powder)
50 g/3½ tablespoons butter
½ teaspoon sea salt
snipped chives, to serve (optional)

SERVES 4

Place the red pepper, cabbage, carrot, onion, chocho and okra in a large saucepan with the bouillon, butter, salt and 75 ml/⅓ cup water. Set over a medium heat and sauté, stirring continuously, for 5–10 minutes until the vegetables are soft.

Serve the sautéed vegetables hot, garnished with chives if liked.

JERK-SPICED RICE WITH PINEAPPLE

One day I was eating plain rice, and then I just decided to give it a bit more spice. I hunted in a cupboard for jerk marinade, mixed it into my rice and it was one of the best things I ever did! Now I won't enter the big debate about whether rice can actually be jerked, but I would say firmly that rice can be spiced, and is done so heavily within Mediterranean culture. I would also say that jerk is heavily about the use of pimento berries – you can mix many spices together but it's the pimentos that give it its distinction. Jerk-spiced rice draws on both of these theories and is a favourite at Paradise Cove.

This recipe tastes significantly better with my own marinade, which is less salty than typical shop-bought jerk marinades. However, it's all down to personal taste. If you fancy more kick... add more marinade in small increments.

450 g/2⅔ cups basmati rice
40 ml/2½ tablespoons vegetable oil
½ teaspoon sea salt
1 tablespoon good-quality vegetable bouillon or stock powder (I use Marigold vegetable stock powder)
½ x 400-g/14-oz. can of coconut milk
100 g/3½ oz. canned or fresh pineapple, peeled if fresh and chopped into chunks
150 g/5½ oz. Chef Tee's Simple Jerk Marinade (see page 16)

TO SERVE
snipped chives
lime wedges, for squeezing

SERVES 6–12

Wash the rice in a bowl of water, rinse and drain. Do this three times to remove any dirt and take away the starch from the rice.

Place the rice in a large saucepan set over a low heat, along with the oil, salt, bouillon, coconut milk and 750ml/3¼ cups water. Bring to the boil, then cover the pan with a lid and simmer on the lowest setting possible for 20–40 minutes. When the coconut rice is fully cooked and fluffy, take the pan off the heat and set aside.

In a separate pan, lightly sauté the pineapple chunks with the Jerk Marinade until the pineapple is soft. Depending on the size of the chunks, this should take about 10 minutes. Fresh pineapple will take longer to soften, whereas canned will only take a few minutes.

Once cooked, add the warm jerked pineapple and the cooking juices to the rice and stir together well. Serve garnished with chives and throw in a couple of lime wedges for squeezing.

SWEET POTATO FRIES

Like the Caribbean, myself and my style of food have been touched by British influences in some ways. It wouldn't be right in this book, if I didn't demonstrate one of these slight culture crossovers. A chunky-cut Jamican sweet potato, roasted and eaten with an English Sunday roast is simply heaven... and dipping sauces only add to that. 'With all the dipping sauces' my friend Tina would say when ordering! This is definitely one of the side dishes I recommend that you try.

3 large sweet potatoes, unpeeled and chopped into chunky fries
1 teaspoon sea salt
1 bulb of garlic, cloves separated, skin left on and lightly crushed
½ bunch of fresh thyme, sprigs snapped in half
olive oil, for drizzling
dips of your choice, to serve

SERVES 4–8

Preheat the oven to 220°C fan/245°C/475°F/gas 9.

Add the potatoes to a large saucepan. Cover them entirely with water and add the salt – this helps to remove the starch. Boil over a high heat for about 5–10 minutes. You will know the potatoes are done when the water starts to foam (or the water begins a rolling boil). The fries should be soft but still firm to the touch.

Remove from the heat and drain the fries, washing them in cold water using a sieve. This stops the fries overcooking.

Transfer the fries to a roasting tin and add the garlic and thyme. Drizzle with olive oil until the fries are well coated, then add 50 ml/3½ tablespoons water.

Cover the roasting tin with foil, then roast in the preheated oven for 30–40 minutes until the fries are soft and slightly charred. If the potatoes are not charred after 30 minutes, remove the foil, return them to the oven and let them crisp. Serve hot and enjoy with your favourite dipping sauces.

SIMPLE SWEET POTATO MASH

I love sweet potatoes. They are expensive and not always in season, but when you get a good, orange-fleshed, red-skinned one, it tastes divine. They are great on their own and can be the main star of a dish. Here I have made them into a delicious side dish, which for me is an amazing go-to paired with coleslaw.

4 large sweet potatoes (use the
   orange Jamaican ones if possible)

TO SERVE
drizzle of olive oil
sea salt and freshly ground
   black pepper
snipped chives (optional)

SERVES 6–8

Preheat the oven to 220°C fan/245°C/475°F/gas 9.

Pierce the sweet potatoes all over with a fork and wrap them individually in foil. Roast the potatoes in the preheated oven for 30–40 minutes until soft and slightly scorched.

Remove the potatoes from the oven, unwrap, being careful of the escaping steam, and slice the potatoes in half. Use a spoon to scoop out the potato flesh into a bowl and use a potato masher or fork to mash the potatoes until creamy. Serve as it is, or with a drizzle of olive oil, a sprinkle of salt and pepper and garnished with chives, if liked.

NOTES

★ If you are short on time, you can also pierce the potatoes and microwave them for 10–15 minutes on high instead of roasting in the oven.

★ Sweet potatoes can come in a range of colours – purple, silver, orange and red – and can either be orange or white on the inside. Traditionally, Caribbeans use with orange-fleshed sweet potatoes as they are often sweeter; although a white-fleshed one would work just the same.

TRINIDADIAN MAC & CHEESE

I have always said my cooking tells a story, and this recipe is pulled from a range of people. This dish is inspired by my aunt Julie who is a mac-and-cheese queen, and then a chef named Adam James who taught me how to make a creamy mac and cheese. If I am correct, I am sure he was also the one who gave me the pumpkin idea.

This recipe works with an instant cheese sauce, and once upon a time was made with exactly that, but as I grew in my cooking confidence, I learned that the trick with not splitting a cheese sauce, is to simply keep your heat really low as you cook.

300 g/10½ oz. dried macaroni
150 g/5½ oz. butternut squash, peeled, deseeded and diced
1 teaspoon sea salt, for the pasta water

CHEESE SAUCE
200 ml/generous ¾ cup milk
250 g/½ cup grated Cheddar cheese
50 ml/3½ tablespoons condensed milk
30 ml/2 tablespoons vegetable oil
½ tablespoon good-quality vegetable bouillon or stock powder (I use Marigold vegetable stock powder)
freshly ground black pepper, to serve
snipped chives, to garnish

SERVES 6–8

Cook the pasta and the butternut squash together in a large saucepan of salted boiling water over a high heat for 15–20 minutes until al dente. Once cooked, drain and set aside. For best results, rinse under cold running water to stop the pasta cooking any further.

To make the cheese sauce, put the milk in a saucepan set over a low heat until it simmers. Once it starts to bubble, add the grated cheese, condensed milk, oil and bouillon. Continue to simmer over a low heat, stirring, until the cheese has melted and the sauce has thickened and can coat the back of a spoon. For the best results, whisk it, rather than use a spoon and keep doing so until it is creamy. If the sauce begins to split, take it off the heat. This should take about 15 minutes in total.

Once you have a cheese sauce of your desired thickness, add the pasta and butternut squash, mixing it all together, and serve straight away topped with plenty of black pepper and snipped chives, if liked.

NOTE *Alternatively, you can bake the mac and cheese in an oven preheated to 180°C fan/200°C/400°F/gas 6 for 20 minutes with some extra cheese on top for a crispier baked version.*

CLASSIC FRIED DUMPLINGS

Through writing this cookbook I have realized that this is my favourite dish. Truly. Here's why:

My mum died when I was 8 years old, and when I eat this dish I'm taken back to being in my nan's house in Croydon. I am about 4 years old, in dungarees with a gold bracelet on my wrist. One arm clinging to my mum's side and the other stuffing my face with a fried dumpling for breakfast. I can taste the crispy, fried outer layer, and then the soft, lightly salted inside. Then time moves quickly forward to when I am 8 and I had just discovered that you could remove the centre of the dumpling. Meaning you could have the inside with more salty, creamy butter, and then have the hollow, crispy fried dumpling shell stuffed with the wonders of a breakfast dish – a bit of egg and of course the beans and plantain. If we were feeling ambitious, you could even add a bit of sausage for one of the greatest flavour combinations ever!

Dumplings take time to master. I am impatient and burn them when shallow-frying, so I think deep-frying is a better method. When I worked in Brixton, I learned how to make them in a deep-fat fryer by watching a chef named Shelly. We worked the breakfast shift together and I would watch her making them. I also recall opening my new vegan branch and teaching 10 members of staff how to make them – I thought I had come full circle.

When I went to Jamaica, to a small bay called Paradise Cove, every morning I would eat plates and plates of good, well-flavoured food, but nothing would give me more joy than when they served me fried dumplings. Which, as you can imagine, I quickly stuffed with eggs, beans and plantain. Immediately, I was 4 years old again… right by my mum's side.

600 g/4½ cups self-raising/
   self-rising flour
30 ml/2 tablespoons vegetable oil,
   plus extra for shallow frying
60 g/¼ cup granulated sugar
100 ml/generous ⅓ cup milk

**MAKES ABOUT 10 LARGE DUMPLINGS
(OR 16 SMALL)**

Place the flour in a large mixing bowl.

Combine the oil, sugar, milk and 300 ml/1¼ cups water in a jug/pitcher and stir together until the sugar has dissolved.

Slowly add the liquid mixture to the flour, bit by bit, and mix and knead until the mixture is sticky and comes together into a dough. Leave the dough in the bowl, covered with a dish towel, and place in the fridge to set for 4 hours. You can use it immediately if you are short on time, however the time in the fridge gives the gluten a chance to develop and creates a better texture.

When you are ready to fry, pull off golf ball-sized pieces of dough and gently roll them into small balls, indenting the middle of each one with your thumb.

Heat a shallow pan with oil about 2.5 cm/1 in. deep to about 160°C/325°F if you have a thermometer. Otherwise, to check the oil is hot enough, flick a little water into the oil; if the oil spits back at you, it is hot enough to continue. Fry the dumplings in batches for a couple of minutes on each side, until they are cooked and golden brown all over. Be careful not to fry the dumplings on too high a heat, as this will cook the outside and leave a raw batter inside – usually the indent in the middle helps alleviate this. Remove from the pan with a slotted spoon and drain any excess oil on a plate lined with paper towels.

JAMAICAN FESTIVALS

Like dumplings, I love Jamaican festivals. Sweet crispy dumplings with a splash of vanilla – utter heaven! In recent years, you can now buy a ready-made packet mixture, that you just add water to. But if you're old fashioned like me you will want to make it by hand. The trick is to let the dough rest for the gluten to develop, so your festivals have a nice bite to them without a short texture.

150 g/1 cup cornmeal/polenta
300 g/2¼ cups self-raising/
    self-rising flour
75 g/generous ½ cup plain/
    all-purpose flour
75 g/generous ⅓ cup granulated
    sugar
40 ml/2½ tablespoons vanilla
    extract/essence
½ teaspoon sea salt
vegetable oil, for shallow-frying

**MAKES ABOUT 10 LARGE FESTIVALS
(OR 16 SMALL)**

Place the cornmeal and both flours in a large mixing bowl and add the sugar, vanilla extract, salt and 300 ml/1¼ cups water. Mix and knead until the ingredients come together into a dough. Be careful not to overwork the dough as this will cause the mixture to become tight. Cover the dough in the bowl with a clean dish towel and leave in the fridge overnight for the gluten to set.

When you are ready to fry, pull off palm-sized pieces of the dough and gently roll them into small sausage shapes, about 8–10 cm/3¼–4 in. long.

Heat a shallow pan with oil about 2.5 cm/1 in. deep to about 180°C/350°F if you have a thermometer. Otherwise, to check the oil is hot enough, flick a little water into the oil; if the oil spits back at you, it is hot enough to continue. Working in batches, fry the festivals for 6–10 minutes, turning them as needed, until golden brown all over. Remove from the pan with a slotted spoon and drain any excess oil on a plate lined with paper towels.

CAKES & DESSERTS

SWEET TREATS FULL OF MEMORIES

Everyone knows nothing beats granny's cakes! These cakes are simply a staple part of the Sunday family meal – the one meal of the week that brings us all together. Simplistically, they are just the sweet things to end a savoury meal, but culturally they are perhaps the most important part of Caribbean bonding. I've lost count of the amount of times I would stand by my nan's side and watch her shred her carrots and beat her eggs at our house. These were the times I saw her softer side. There were no instructions, merely an unspoken silence where I watched and learned. Where we bonded. Life was hard, but through cooking, I could see a happiness that was elsewhere found...

During my teen years, baking was a way to express myself. I recall finding a Good Housekeeping cookbook in my early teens and teaching myself how to make scones or a simple Victoria sponge. And by the time I was in my teens and purchased a food processor... well this is really where the Paradise Cove story began. I would watch the chefs at work effortlessly flinging their banana cakes in the oven and dance in the kitchen. I studied each of their movements, until I got the knack myself. I think I was 17 when I remember saying I wanted to own a restaurant, and these recipes here are the first ones I created.

Baking is a science so it's always good to be precise, but also remember why you're doing it... forget your worries, do it with your children and nieces and nephews, create something tasty together, but most importantly, create a memory that lasts forever.

Fishermen boats docked on the
White River in St Ann, Jamaica.

BANANA CAKE

After my rum bread pudding, this was one of the first recipes I ever created for my restaurant. The moral of the story is never give up. The second moral is to use ripe, almost entirely black bananas. The third is to not overmash the bananas... if you do that, you risk overworking the mixture, which will create dense, under-cooked layers.

butter, for greasing
250 g/generous 1¾ cups
   self-raising/self-rising flour,
   plus extra for dusting
200 g/1 cup granulated sugar
175 ml/¾ cup vegetable oil
1 tablespoon baking powder
3 ripe bananas, mashed
3 eggs
40 ml/2½ tablespoons almond
   extract
1 teaspoon ground allspice
   (or ground nutmeg or cinnamon)

*26-cm/10¼-in. diameter springform
cake tin*

SERVES 8–12

Preheat the oven to 160°C fan/180°C/350°F/gas 4. Line the base of the cake tin with non-stick baking paper. Rub a knob/pat of butter around the edges of the tin, then dust the tin with flour – this helps the mixture climb up the sides of the tin as it rises.

Place all the ingredients in a food processor and pulse for 4 seconds until just evenly combined. If mixing by hand, simply mix all the ingredients together in a mixing bowl until just evenly combined. Pour the mixture into the prepared tin.

Bake in the preheated oven for 40–60 minutes. The cake should be cooked when it is even in colour, however some darker bananas give a cooked appearance when the cake actually needs a bit longer. To check it is cooked, pierce the centre of the cake with a knife or skewer. If the knife or skewer comes out clean, it is fully cooked; if it comes out with mixture still on it, continue baking and repeat the checking process at 10-minute intervals thereafter. Be careful not to keep opening the oven as this lowers the oven temperature though.

Leave to cool in the tin, covered with a wet dish towel to retain moisture. Remove from the tin when cold. For the best results, serve the next day.

NOTES

★ *To make your cake vegan, replace the eggs with 150 g/5½ oz. apple sauce.*

★ *Add pineapple rings to the bottom of the cake tin and then pour the mixture over the top to create a pineapple and banana cake!*

A NOTE ABOUT OVENS

For the best results, use a convection oven and bake with the heat coming from below. A fan oven circulates heat around the cake and can dry the cake out at the top, causing it to crack and dry. If you're using a fan oven, place the cake on the second lowest shelf with a small heat-proof bowl of water on the bottom shelf – a 'bain-marie' if you will – to keep the cake moist. If you still find your cake dries out and is not moist, try baking at a lower temperature. It is all about understanding how your oven works.

QUICK BLACK CAKE

Black cake or Christmas cake is a cake that is festively comparable to British Christmas pudding. Raisins are soaked all year round for it. One of my nan's is from Jamaica and the other is from St Lucia, but both have the same practice of keeping a jar above the fridge, full of raisins, all year round. If you haven't the time to soak raisins all year, but still wish to enjoy the soaking process: you can soak them for about 3 days, then blitz them into a pulp to give the same result. Finally, it is worth noting that Jamaican Red Label wine, isn't a normal red wine, it is an aperitif. English sherry would be the closest comparison by taste. If you can't find it, you can still use red wine — I did in my first ever batch to gain an understanding of Caribbean culture and learned that you can substitute it for a normal red wine; you will just end up with a less sweet cake. If this is the case I would advise using a light-bodied red wine.

300 g/2 cups raisins

150 ml/²⁄₃ cup white rum

100 ml/generous ⅓ cup Red Label Aperitif (or see introduction above for alternatives)

butter, for greasing

250 g/generous 1¾ cups self-raising/self-rising flour, plus extra for dusting

200 g/1 cup granulated sugar

175 ml/¾ cup vegetable oil

1 tablespoon baking powder

2 tablespoons dark soy sauce

3 eggs

40 ml/2½ tablespoons almond extract

1 teaspoon ground allspice (or ground nutmeg or cinnamon)

26-cm/10¼-in. diameter springform cake tin

SERVES 8–12

To prepare the raisins, place the raisins, rum and wine in a small saucepan and boil over a high heat with the lid on until the raisins have absorbed all the alcohol. Set aside in a bowl and leave to cool — if the raisins are too hot, this will cook the cake batter when you are mixing it all together. Once it is cool, add to a food processor and pulse into a pulp.

Preheat the oven to 160°C fan/180°C/350°F/gas 4. Line the base of the cake tin with non-stick baking paper. Rub a knob/pat of butter around the edges of the tin, then dust the tin with flour. This helps the mixture climb up the sides of the tin as it rises.

Add the blitzed raisins and all the remaining ingredients to a food processor and pulse for 4 seconds. If mixing by hand, simply mix everything together in a bowl until all the ingredients are just evenly combined. Scrape the sides down and pulse again for 4 seconds. Pour the mixture into the prepared tin.

Bake in the preheated oven for 1 hour. To check it is cooked, pierce the centre of the cake with a knife or skewer. If the knife or skewer comes out clean, it is fully cooked; if it comes out with mixture still on it, continue baking and repeat the checking process at 10-minute intervals thereafter. Be careful not to keep opening the oven as this lowers the oven temperature though. Leave to cool in the tin, covered with a wet dish towel to retain moisture. Remove from the tin when cold.

NOTE *Traditionally, Jamaican browning sauce is used as a colouring agent, giving this cake its distinctive black colour. However, my preference is to use dark soy sauce, as a good-quality brand will have no MSG and its salt content acts as a flavour enhancer.*

GINGER CAKE

Ginger cake is a staple in the Caribbean. Many shop-bought brands are well-established in this area, and their goods can easily be found in shops over here or in any world food sections of a good supermarket. Using inspiration from my style of baking cakes, I played around with what I knew and simply adapted it to create a ginger cake with natural, high-quality ingredients. Traditionally, ginger cake has a dense and filling texture, whereas my recipe is slightly lighter. It works best with fresh ginger, and for a stronger ginger taste, swap part of the carrots for more ginger, always using at least 100 g/3½ oz. carrots.

butter, for greasing
200 g/1½ cups self-raising/self-rising
   flour, plus extra for dusting
200 g/1 cup granulated sugar
3 large/US extra-large eggs
250 ml/1 cup vegetable oil
2 carrots, peeled and grated
100 g/3½ oz. fresh ginger, grated
1 teaspoon table salt
1½ teaspoons baking powder
pinch of mixed spice
   (or ground cinnamon)
80 g/½ cup raisins

26-cm/10¼-in. diameter springform
   cake tin

SERVES 8–12

Preheat the oven to 160°C fan/180°C/350°F/gas 4. Line the base of the cake tin with non-stick baking paper. Rub a knob/pat of butter around the edges of the tin, then dust the tin with flour. This helps the mixture climb up the sides of the tin as it rises.

Place the sugar, eggs and oil in a food processor and pulse until creamy and thick. Add the remaining ingredients to the food processor and pulse for 4 seconds. Scrape the sides down, then pulse again for 4 seconds until everything is just evenly combined. Pour the mixture into the prepared cake tin.

Bake in the preheated oven for 40–60 minutes. To check it is cooked, pierce the centre of the cake with a knife or skewer. If the knife comes out clean, it is fully cooked; if it comes out with mixture still on it, continue baking and repeat the process at 10-minute intervals. Be careful not to keep opening the oven as this lowers the oven temperature though.

NOTE It is important to always mix the eggs, oil and sugar together first to create a base for the fresh ingredients, or your cake may struggle to rise.

CARROT & WALNUT CAKE

What makes this cake special, is that it's the first cake I ever made with an oil base. By mixing the eggs with the oil and sugar first, you create a base with protein, and this helps to stabilize the loose batter. This method also give you a huge amount of flexibility, allowing you to be heavy handed with your carrots and even change the nuts. Here I have chosen walnuts, but you could opt for almonds or no nuts at all!

butter, for greasing
200 g/1½ cups self-raising/self-
    rising flour, plus extra for dusting
200 g/1 cup granulated sugar
4 eggs
240 ml/1 cup vegetable oil
3 carrots, peeled and grated
1½ teaspoons baking powder
pinch of mixed spice or ground
    cinnamon
100 g/3½ oz. walnuts, crushed,
    plus extra to decorate

CARIBBEAN-INSPIRED BUTTERCREAM
200 g/¾ cup unsalted butter at
    room temperature
2 tablespoons white rum
    or amaretto liqueur
1 tablespoon vanilla extract/essence
70 g/2½ oz. cream cheese
100–200 g/1–1½ cups icing/
    powdered sugar (to taste)
2 tablespoons double/heavy cream

*26-cm/10¼-in. diameter springform
    cake tin*

SERVES 8–12

Preheat the oven to 160°C fan/180°C/350°F/gas 4. Line the base of the cake tin with non-stick baking paper. Rub a knob/pat of butter around the edges of the tin, then dust the tin with flour. This helps the mixture climb up the sides of the tin as it rises.

Place the sugar, eggs and oil in a food processor and pulse until creamy. Add the remaining cake ingredients to the food processor and pulse for 4 seconds. Scrape the sides down, then pulse again for 4 seconds until everything is just evenly combined. Pour the mixture into the prepared tin.

Bake in the preheated oven for 1 hour. To check it is cooked, pierce the centre of the cake with a knife or skewer. If it comes out clean, it is fully cooked; if it comes out with mixture still on it, continue baking and repeat the process at 10-minute intervals. Be careful not to keep opening the oven as this lowers the oven temperature though.

To make the buttercream, put all the ingredients in a food processor and pulse until combined. If the mixture is too wet (loose), add in more icing sugar, 50 g/¼ cup at a time. Spoon the buttercream onto the cake in an ad-hoc fashion (no pattern, just dollop it on in waves). Decorate the iced cake with crushed walnuts.

BEETROOT CAKE

When I was growing up in my twenties, a lot of people became cake makers. Parties, events or gatherings were adorned with cupcakes or more impressive party cakes. Then as time went by and social media gained a bigger influence on our lives, the trend for cakes was 'red velvet'. So many recipes can be found for this cake. Some with buttermilk, some vegan, some gluten-free... the list goes on. But the key to any cake is to maintain its moisture and, of course, its flavour.

Creating an oil-based cake takes practice, but I find it works better than a batter-based one. You can control the moisture and spongy texture more easily, as well as extend its shelf life. Lastly, I find that fresh beetroot works amazingly well with this recipe and gives the cake not only a speckled pink colour, but an earthy taste, only describable as 'Mother Earth'.

butter, for greasing
200 g/1½ cups self-raising/self-rising flour, plus extra for dusting
200 g/1 cup caster/superfine sugar
4 eggs
240 ml/1 cup vegetable oil
1 fresh beetroot/beet, peeled and grated
200 g/1½ cups grated carrot
1½ teaspoons baking powder
1 teaspoon sea salt

26-cm/10¼-in. diameter springform cake tin

SERVES 8–12

Preheat the oven to 160°C fan/180°C/350°F/gas 4. Line the base of the cake tin with non-stick baking paper. Rub a knob/pat of butter around the edges of the tin, then dust the tin with flour. This helps the mixture climb up the sides of the tin as it rises.

Place the sugar, eggs and oil in a food processor and pulse until the mixture is creamy and thick. Add the remaining ingredients and pulse for 4 seconds. Scrape the sides down and pulse again for 4 seconds, until everything is just evenly combined, then pour the mixture into the prepared tin.

Bake in the preheated oven for 1 hour. To check it is cooked, pierce the centre of the cake with a knife or skewer. If the knife or skewer comes out clean, it is fully cooked; if it comes out with mixture still on it, continue baking and repeat the checking process at 10-minute intervals thereafter. Be careful not to keep opening the oven as this lowers the oven temperature though.

Leave to cool in the tin, covered with a wet dish towel to retain moisture. Remove from the tin when cold.

CLASSIC CORNMEAL PORRIDGE

Cornmeal or polenta porridge really did not hold any pleasant memories for me until I was taught to cook it by Shelly (who was a chef I learned from in my Brixton years). It's a slow process that requires patience. If you rush it, you risk undercooking the polenta – which will make you unwell or create a grainy texture. Shelly also taught me the importance of using good-quality products, as you end up with a smoother porridge. Here, I have stylized a recipe with extra sweetness. The chocolate chips, coconut chips and/or dried banana bring the sweetness to my version, but if you wish to be traditional, then cornmeal porridge, simply sweetened with condensed milk, with a bit of hard dough bread on the side, is more than enough to get you going in the morning and line your stomach with fuel for the day.

200 g/1⅓ cups fine cornmeal/
    polenta
150 ml/⅔ cup oat milk
450 ml/scant 2 cups water (or 100 ml/
    scant ½ cup coconut milk mixed
    with 350 ml/1½ cups water)
½ teaspoon sea salt
¼ teaspoon ground nutmeg
60 ml/¼ cup pure vanilla extract/
    essence
condensed milk, molasses or honey,
    to taste (optional)
coconut chips, chocolate chips and/
    or fresh or dried banana,
    to decorate (optional)

SERVES 4

Place the cornmeal, oat milk and water in a small saucepan set over a low heat and whisk for about 10 minutes until thick in consistency. Whisk the salt, nutmeg and vanilla extract into the porridge.

Take the pan off the heat and add the condensed milk, molasses or honey. Taste to check the sweetness and add more if needed.

Return the pan back to the heat over the lowest setting, and continue to whisk for about 10 minutes until the porridge produces thick bubbles. The porridge should have a smooth and slightly grainy texture – found with cornmeal-based products. If the porridge is chalky in its texture, it means the cornmeal hasn't finished cooking and needs more time and whisking.

Top with coconut chips, chocolate chips, banana and/or extra honey to serve if liked.

NOTE *This porridge gets thicker with time, so after you cook it, discard any leftovers. It isn't nice reheated or eaten on another day.*

ANNETTE'S FRUIT SALAD WITH COCONUT TOAST

My aunty Annette taught me so much – how to live, how to be a young man, to be grateful for life. She nearly taught me this recipe, but instead, having taught me to be grateful, she didn't need to teach it to me, because I remember it. I remember hearing the clink of the crystal bowl she served it in. I remember watching her fill the bowl with lashings and lashings of condensed milk, smelling the fresh fruits. Not a dish that I had ever seen before, but one that is sensational in flavour. So much of my exposure to Caribbean culture and food began with Annette – things like bammy, fish, bully beef were the norm in her house – and this is one of those dishes. I've modernized it with a twist I picked up in Jamaica and I hope it brings you as much joy as it brings me.

100 g/3½ oz. grapes, chopped
100 g/3½ oz. strawberries, chopped
100 g/3½ oz. blueberries
2 apples, peeled, cored and chopped
1 mango, peeled, stoned/pitted
   and chopped
50 g/⅓ cup raisins
1 orange, peeled and chopped
1 banana, peeled and chopped
50 g/1¾ oz. cherries, stoned/pitted
50 g/1¾ oz. crushed walnuts
1 teaspoon ground allspice
   (or nutmeg or cinnamon)
½ x 400-g/14-oz. can of condensed
   milk
250 ml/1 cup double/heavy cream
40 ml/2½ tablespoons vanilla
   extract/essence

COCONUT TOAST
4 large/US extra-large eggs
½ teaspoon ground allspice
   (or nutmeg or cinnamon)
100 ml/generous ⅓ cup milk
4 slices of bread
1 teaspoon desiccated coconut
knob/pat of butter, for frying

SERVES 2–4

Place all of the fruit, nuts and allspice in a large mixing bowl and mix together until combined.

Mix the condensed milk, cream and vanilla extract together in a separate bowl until combined. Pour the cream mixture over the fruit, cover the bowl and leave in the fridge until ready to serve.

To make the coconut toasts, mix the eggs, allspice and milk together in a bowl. Dip the slices of bread in the egg mixture, making sure they are well coated on both sides.

Melt the butter in a frying pan/skillet over a medium heat, then carefully place 1–2 eggy bread slices in the pan. Sprinkle the bread with desiccated coconut, before flipping and sprinkling with more coconut. Cook for 4–6 minutes until the bread is golden in colour on both sides. Repeat the frying process with the remaining eggy bread slices and coconut, adding more butter to the pan as needed.

Cut the coconut toasts into triangles and serve with a generous helping of fruit salad.

JAMAICAN-INSPIRED TOTO BITES WITH RUM CUSTARD

Visiting Jamaica, I came across toto cake. A coconut cake with a similar taste to coconut drops – another Caribbean treat. I am not normally a coconut person but once upon a time when I was cooking from home, I created a spin-off dessert brand called Blue Mountain, inspired by the foods and flavours that would go with Blue Mountain coffee. This lead me to look back at some of my earlier creations to give my desserts the originality of the classics, but with the uniqueness of new ideas.

I love cookie dough and nothing ever beats homemade custard – so here I combined all the things I love. Inspired by Jamaica, Blue Mountain coffee, alcohol and comfort, you have everything to finish off your winter in total comfort.

TOTO BITES
100 g/1⅓ cups desiccated/dried shredded coconut
300 g/1½ cups granulated sugar
80 g/3 oz. chocolate chips
300 g/2¼ cups plain/all-purpose flour
80 ml/⅓ cup vanilla extract/essence

RUM CUSTARD
300 ml/1¼ cups oat or dairy milk
50 ml/3½ tablespoons single/light cream
½ teaspoon vanilla extract/essence
2–3 egg yolks
60 g/scant ⅓ cup caster/superfine sugar
2 teaspoons plain/all-purpose flour
60 ml/¼ cup white rum

SERVES 4–6

First, make the toto bites. Place all the ingredients in a bowl and mix into a dough.

Roll the dough mixture into small walnut-sized balls and set on a baking tray lined with baking paper. Transfer to the fridge and leave to set for 2 hours in the fridge or 1 hours in the freezer.

Next, make the custard. Put the milk and cream in a saucepan set over a low heat and whisk until it starts to simmer. Add the vanilla extract.

Whisk the egg yolks, sugar and flour together in a separate bowl until combined.

Pour the hot milk mixture into the egg mixture, whisking continuously until combined. Pour the custard mix back into the saucepan and set it back over a low heat. Gently stir with a wooden spatula for about 6–10 minutes until thickened, then stir in the rum.

Put the toto bites in a bowl and serve with the hot custard.

PUNCHES, COCKTAILS & JUICES

LIQUID JOY TO ENHANCE ANY MEAL

There are just so many Caribbean drinks that could be in this section – carrot juice, sorrel, sour sop, peanut punch – the list goes on! Some of the recipes that appear here are things that I grew up with, others are ones that I have created over time and some are ones I found on the island of Jamaica!

Unlike the other sections in this book, here I use the entirety of my kitchen's cooking equipment and blend, heat, crush, freeze, juice and sieve to create these beverages.

Rum (which is made from sugarcane) is heavily featured in this section as it is synonymous with the Caribbean. You will find it can be added sparingly or heavily to your drinks – it's all about personal taste. With that being said, this section also features the use of cloves, mixed spice and ginger, which are powerful in taste so need careful measuring.

It took a lot of mixology practice to understand that no two drink batches will be identical, so have fun and enjoy tasting as you go.

Above left: Traditional colourful bamboo
outdoor cook shop on Winnifred Beach,
Jamaica. Above right: Caribbean beach
in Saona island, Dominican Republic.

SIMPLE RUM PUNCH

Nothing beats a classic rum punch. There are hundreds of ways to make it — shop-bought, secret family recipes, local recipes and recipes from friends. Everyone has their own particular way of mixing up a rum punch. There really are no hard and fast rules, so use this as a guide, however keep in mind that you are ultimately aiming to have a pink-to-reddish colour drink at the end. Also, I'd recommend including pimento berries and ginger as this gives Caribbean rum punch its signature distinctive flavour, which elevates it from the usual punches I have tasted before.

125 ml/½ cup strong white rum
50 ml/scant ¼ cup good-quality orange juice
500 ml/2 cups cranberry juice
250 ml/1 cup good-quality mango juice
50 ml/scant ¼ cup grenadine (or 50 g/¼ cup caster/superfine sugar)
thumb-sized piece of fresh ginger, peeled and grated
1 teaspoon pimento berries, crushed
ice cubes

OPTIONAL FRESH FRUITS
strawberries, hulled and sliced
pomegranate seeds
glacé cherries
pineapple chunks
orange slices
lime slices
lemon slices

SERVES 4

Mix the rum and all the fruit juices together in a large jug/pitcher. Stir the grenadine or sugar, ginger and pimento berries into the punch mix. Serve in tall glasses with several ice cubes and fresh fruit of your choice.

NOTE *Alternatively, if you wish to make the punch into a slushy, then use a blender to blend all the ingredients together with several ice cubes.*

PUMPKIN PUNCH

A few years into opening my restaurant, I decided that I wanted to try some Halloween specials. I cracked this pumpkin punch using my Guinness punch as a base. It's an orange punch that tastes of pumpkin, sweetness and stout!

200 g/7 oz. pumpkin, peeeld and
    chopped into chunks
200 g/7 oz. butternut squash,
    skin on and chopped into chunks
1 x 440-ml/15-fl. oz. can of Irish dry
    stout, such as Guinness
60 ml/¼ cup dark rum
1 x 400-g/14-oz can of vanilla-
    flavoured high-protein drink
    (see Notes below)
60 ml/¼ cup vanilla extract/essence
½ x 400-g/14-oz. can of condensed
    milk
½ teaspoon ground cinnamon
ice cubes
cocoa powder or ground nutmeg,
    for dusting

SERVES 6

Preheat the oven to 180°C fan/200°C/400°F/gas 6.

Place the pumpkin and squash in a roasting tin, cover with foil and roast in the preheated oven for 20–40 minutes until cooked and soft. Leave to cool.

Once the roasted veg has cooled, add it to a food processor or blender. Add the remaining ingredients with several ice cubes and blend until smooth. Pour into a jug/pitcher and serve in tall glasses with a dusting of cocoa powder or nutmeg.

NOTES

★ *Sweeten to taste with further condensed milk If needed.*

★ *If you cannot get hold of vanilla-flavoured high-protein drink, you can substitute with 340 ml/1⅓ cups full-fat/whole milk mixed with 60 ml/¼ cup vanilla extract/essence.*

BANANA & NUT SMOOTHIE

Variations of peanut punches and smoothies are found all over the islands of the Caribbean. They are often made with monkey nuts, tasting buttery and alcoholic and are delicious, refreshing and slightly addictive. With a bit of determination I have come up with my own unique take on peanut punch, as I always knew it was something I wanted to include in this book. For me, I love the surprise that comes from the crunch of a peanut in this punch, so I prefer to use crunchy peanut butter for optimal texture.

2 peeled and frozen bananas
300–500 ml/1¼–2 cups almond
   or oat milk
3 tablespoons crunchy peanut butter
squeeze of honey or agave syrup
60–120 ml/¼–½ cup white rum
   of your choice (optional)
ice cubes
cocoa powder or grated nutmeg,
   to serve

SERVES 4–6

Place all the ingredients in a food processor or blender with several ice cubes and blend until smooth. Pour into a jug/pitcher and serve with a dusting of cocoa powder or nutmeg.

NOTE *Bananas should be peeled, placed in a food bag and frozen overnight before using here. If you don't have any prepared, the punch will work the same when blended with fresh bananas and extra ice cubes.*

GUINNESS PUNCH

There is an amazing Caribbean shop in Brixton, London, which sells the most incredible Guinness punch. It's served all year round but can often be found at special events close to Christmas time. I would visit this shop frequently as they were the only Caribbean shop that could make the punch as good as my nan! The drink is delicious in taste, creamy, warming and sweet with a hint of stout. For best results, I'd advise using the exact ingredients listed here, but if they are unavailable, feel free to use suitable substitutes (see Note below).

1–2 x 440-ml/15-fl. oz. cans of Irish dry stout, such as Guinness (2 cans creates a stronger flavour)
1 x 400-g/14-oz. can of vanilla-flavoured high-protein drink (see Note below)
60 ml/¼ cup vanilla extract/essence
½ x 400-g/14-oz. can of condensed milk (more can be added for a sweeter flavour)
½ teaspoon ground allspice, cinnamon or nutmeg, plus extra to decorate
ice cubes

SERVES 2

Place all the ingredients in a food processor or blender with a handful of ice cubes and blitz until combined. Serve in tall glasses over more ice with extra condensed milk, if needed, and a dusting of extra allspice, cinnamon or nutmeg to decorate.

NOTES

★ The mixture will split when left to stand, so will need stirring occasionally if serving from a jug.

★ If you cannot get hold of vanilla-flavoured high-protein drink, you can substitute with 400 ml/1⅔ cups oat milk mixed with 60 ml/¼ cup vanilla extract/essence.

CARIBBEAN KING MOCKTAIL

There is a reason this cocktail has the name 'king' and that is because it's not for the faint-hearted. You have to chop a green coconut and that is no easy task. Coconuts aren't easy to open, so I would always say to be mindful while doing this – see the Note below for instructions – but you should know that all the effort will be worth it as nothing beats fresh coconut water.

1 mango, peeled, stoned/pitted and
   chopped
100 g/3½ oz. papaya, peeled, stoned/
   pitted and chopped
juice and jelly of 1 green jelly
   coconut (see Note below)
1 orange, peeled and chopped
juice of ¼ lime

SERVES 1–2

Freeze the mango and papaya for 2–4 hours until completely frozen.

Remove from the freezer and put in a food processor or blender. Add the fresh juice and jelly of a green jelly coconut, the chopped orange and lime juice. Blend until mixed to a slushy consistency, then serve in tall glasses.

NOTE *The green jelly coconut will require chopping with a sharp knife. Chop the green skin off until the three marks of the husk begin to show. It should look like a bowling ball. Pierce to release the juice. If you don't feel confident doing this, or can't get hold of it, you can swap with 100 ml/⅓ cup shop-bought coconut water and a tablespoon of coconut milk.*

WATERMELON SPLASH MOCKTAIL

I love watermelon. There is something about its refreshing quality. I can't think of a better fruit!

400 g/14 oz. watermelon,
   plus wedges to decorate
200 ml/generous ¾ cup chilled guava juice
juice of 2 limes
100 ml/generous ⅓ cup passion fruit juice
caster/superfine sugar, for rimming
1 passion fruit, halved, to decorate

SERVES 2

Peel and chop the watermelon, no need to deseed, and freeze for 2–4 hours until completely frozen.

Put the frozen watermelon in a food processor or blender with the guava, lime and passion fruit juices and blend until combined to a slushy texture.

Rim 2 glasses with sugar and pour in the mocktail. Decorate with passion fruit halves and a wedge of watermelon each.

BOB MARLEY COCKTAIL

You can't go to Jamaica and not have a Bob Marley. It's a simple cocktail that is quite strong but looks stunning due to the different liquid densities. The liquids float on top of each other creating a layered effect. And the colours do nothing but make you smile – similar to the man the drink is named after!

When making this cocktail, go for good-quality brands – particularly when choosing your rum!

crushed ice
35 ml/2 tablespoons grenadine
50 ml/3½ tablespoons pineapple
   and coconut juice
50 ml/3½ tablespoons mango juice
30 ml/2 tablespoons white rum
35 ml/2 tablespoons spiced pineapple
   rum or another yellow, flavoured
   alcohol (passion fruit gin works well)
35 ml/2 tablespoons blue curaçao
fruit of your choice and/or pineapple
   leaves, to decorate

SERVES 1

Fill a tall glass with crushed ice and add the grenadine – this creates the red layer.

Mix the pineapple and coconut juice, mango juice and white rum in a Boston shaker, then add to the glass, creating the yellow layer. Add more ice to your glass if needed at this point.

Mix the spiced rum or gin and blue curaçao in a Boston shaker, then carefully pour this into the glass to create the final blue layer. Decorate with fruit and/ or some pineapple leaves if you have them and serve.

LYCHEE & WATERMELON DAIQUIRI

When my restaurant changed from BYOB to fully licenced, this was one of my summer creations. Before, customers would bring bottles of rum and we would turn them into slushies, but when the restaurant changed, I wanted to recreate the slushy on the menu. You will find stronger alcohol will lower the freezing point of ice, and therefore melt your drink slightly. You won't know until you try, but to fix this problem if it arises, pour the mix back into the blender with 1–2 extra ice cubes. Blend it again and serve.

400 g/14 oz. watermelon, peeled
   and chopped
5–10 lychees, peeled
60 ml/¼ cup alcohol of your choice
   (white rum works best)
juice of 2 limes
200 g/7 oz. ice cubes
fruit juice of your choice, if needed
   to loosen the mix (optional)
fine sea salt, for rimming

SERVES 2–3

Freeze the watermelon for 2–4 hours until completely frozen.

Put the lychees, frozen watermelon, alcohol and lime juice in a food processor or blender with ice cubes and blend into a slushy. If the mix won't blend easily, add a fruit juice of your choice (50 ml/ 3½ tablespoons at a time) to help loosen the mix.

Rim glasses with salt and pour in the slushy mix.

CARIBBEAN BOLT

In the Caribbean we love carrot juice. It's a juice made with love and a lot of labour. To do it right, you have to do it by hand. Grating the carrots, and then straining the juice, then adding spices, then adding condensed milk. It's not something you use a juicer for.

When I opened our vegan branch, I wanted something that encapsulated this essence without too much labour intensity. With this version, you will find the blended ice cubes give the drink substantial body, with the fruits and reduced amount of condensed milk adding the right amount of sweetness.

4 oranges, peeled
1 pineapple, peeled
10 large carrots, peeled
several ice cubes
pinch of ground allspice,
   cinnamon or nutmeg
60 ml/¼ cup condensed milk
   (optional)

juicer

SERVES 2

Use a juicer to extract the juice from the oranges, pineapple and carrots.

Add the juices to a food processor or blender with some ice cubes, the allspice, cinnamon or nutmeg and the condensed milk, if using. Blend to a slushy consistency and pour into glasses to serve.

NOTE *Condensed milk is traditionally used to thicken and sweeten juices in the Caribbean, but it's not vital here, if you would rather leave it out. The ice cubes will do the job of thickening the smoothie when blended.*

BANANA JOY SMOOTHIE

With the opening of my vegan branch I began exploring ital ways of making the much-loved dairy dishes and popular drinks that you all had become so accustomed to.

I love this drink. The espresso makes it mature enough for any adult, but take it away and you are left with a fun, child-friendly smoothie. The most amazing thing is how the frozen banana, once blended, gives this drink a thick smoothie texture. In my opinion, it's definitely one of the top drinks in this chapter.

1 peeled and frozen banana
250 ml/1 cup almond milk
1 shot of espresso
a couple of ice cubes
cocoa powder or grated nutmeg,
   to serve

SERVES 1

Blend all the ingredients in a food processor or blender until smooth. Pour into a tall glass and serve with a dusting of cocoa powder or nutmeg.

NOTE *A ripe banana works best, so something yellow to partially black. Anything else will taste too ripe or won't be soft enough to blend well.*

TERRE-DE-BAS EGGNOG

I adore eggnog. It's not commonly found in the UK so it is a bit of a treat. This recipe I have had since I was 18, and without fail it's one I make every year for myself. The lychees are optional but add something different if serving this drink cold. It doesn't sound like it would work, but it certainly does.

3 large/US extra-large eggs
500 ml/2 cups oat, almond
   or dairy milk
30–50 g/2–3½ tablespoons caster/
   superfine sugar, to taste
30 ml/2 tablespoons vanilla extract/
   essence (or seeds from 1 vanilla
   pod/bean)
¼ teaspoon ground cinnamon
   or 1 cinnamon stick (optional)
100 ml/generous ⅓ cup amaretto
   liqueur or rum (or 60 ml/¼ cup
   whisky)

IF SERVING WARM
whipped cream
cocoa powder
icing/powdered sugar

IF SERVING COLD
3–5 large lychees, peeled

SERVES 4–6

Place the eggs, milk, sugar, vanilla and cinnamon in a saucepan and heat over a low heat. Cook for 2–3 minutes, stirring, until the mixture is combined and loosely coats the back of a wooden spoon. If you prefer a slightly thicker eggnog, cook while stirring for a few minutes longer. Add the alcohol and stir through before removing from the heat.

If serving warm, pour into mugs and add the whipped cream and a dusting of cocoa powder and icing sugar. If serving cold, leave to cool and serve over ice with some peeled lychees.

NOTE *For a richer eggnog, use 4 egg yolks instead of 3 large eggs.*

FESTIVE SORREL

For me, sorrel punch is the Jamaican equivalent of mulled wine – it's red, served at Christmas and infused with spices. It took me a long time to come round to sorrel as I didn't really like cloves. I also had to understand what makes it 'authentically' sorrel. As I dislike cloves, I have made these optional, but they are a part of this drink's 'authenticity', so I would advise trying the full recipe before making changes.

100–200 g/3½–7 oz. Jamaican
   dried sorrel (hibiscus flowers)
40–60 g/1½–2 oz. fresh ginger,
   peeled and chopped for a
   weaker flavour or grated
   for stronger flavour
1 cinnamon stick
½ tablespoon pimento berries
½ teaspoon cloves (optional)
2 oranges
1 lime
1 lemon
150–300 g/¾–1½ cups
   granulated sugar

TO SERVE
1 orange, sliced
thumb-sized piece of fresh ginger,
   peeled and grated (optional)
cinnamon stick (optional)
ice cubes

SERVES 6–8

Boil 1.8 litres/7½ cups water in a large saucepan over a low heat and add the sorrel, ginger, cinnamon stick, pimento berries and cloves, if using. Quarter all of the citrus fruits, squeeze in the juice and drop the wedges into the pan too. Continue cooking over a low heat for 1 hour for the flavours to infuse.

Remove from the heat and add sugar to taste. The more ginger you have used, the more you may want to sweeten your drink. Strain the infused mixture into a jug/pitcher. Add the sliced orange, grated ginger and cinnamon, if liked, and leave to cool to room temperature. Serve over ice.

NOTE *To make this punch alcoholic, add 125–250 ml/½–1 cup white rum (or more for a stronger taste).*

GLOSSARY OF CARIBBEAN FOOD

ACKEE A savoury fruit with a thick red skin, grown on evergreen trees and used abundantly in Jamaican cooking, most notably in Jamaica's national dish of Ackee and Saltfish (see page 52).

AGAVE Some times known as maguey syrup. A vegan-friendly syrup produced from the agave plant, this natural sweetener is similar in its properties to golden syrup or honey and great for sweetening drinks.

ALLSPICE Also known as Jamaican pepper, this is the dried unripe berry of the Pimenta dioica tree. It is a warming spice used in a lot of Caribbean cooking.

BANANA BLOSSOM A tear-shaped flower with purple skin that grows at the end of a cluster of bananas. When eaten raw, it is an ideal replacement for fish in terms of texture, or can be cooked.

BEANS (FRESH YOUNG) Sometimes called baby limas, they have a thin skin surrounding a pale green bean that can be removed after cooking or left intact, depending on the how they are being used. Mature, dried butter beans have a thicker, beige-coloured skin that becomes tender when fully cooked.

BELL PEPPERS Bell peppers are large palm-sized peppers from the Capsicum annuum family, named bell after their distinctive bell shape. In the UK they are commonly called sweet peppers for their sweet, not spicy, taste. Bell peppers are used most frequently in salads but can be used in a range of dishes for texture, colour or flavour.

BETAPAC This is a Jamaican curry powder that I use a lot in my cooking. It has the perfect blend of spices for me, but you can use any other madras curry powder if you can't get hold of it.

BLACK BEANS The black turtle bean is a bean originally from South America. Its hard outer shell gives it its 'turtle' name and dense meaty texture has made it a great plant-based staple. It's commonly used in plant-based burgers or stews.

BLUE CURAÇAO A liqueur made from the dried peel of the bitter orange larva, which is a citrus fruit grown on the island of Curaçao and used in many Caribbean cocktails.

BROWNING A traditional colouring agent made from molasses. This often contains MSG – which is an artificial colouring agent. Although traditional, I prefer to use dark soy sauce, which can be gluten and vegan friendly.

BUTTER BEANS A larger than normal bean that originated in South America and can also be known as lima beans. They're available fresh during the late-summer or found canned in any good supermarket. Within the Caribbean they are most commonly used in Oxtail dishes.

CALLALOO A green leafy vegetable from the amaranth family. Its tender leaves are incredibly nutritious and are delicious sautéed or when added to other dishes. Spinach can be used as an alternative.

CASSAVA A root vegetable that is part of the cassava shrub. While its leaves are more often used in African cuisine, its roots are often used in Caribbean cooking. Rich in carbohydrates, it is commonly used in soups and stews and breads – such as bammy (see page 43).

CHIVES A flowering plant that is part of the Allium genus family. It is commonly used as a garnishing herb with a mild onion taste. It is great for curries and other spiced dishes rather than parsley or coriander due to its lighter taste.

CHOCHO/CHAYOTE – an oval-shaped Jamaican fruit used mostly in salads, pickles, soups and stews.

CINNAMON A spice from the bark of trees. Often use in sweet dishes and is interchangeable with mixed spice. Not to be confused with allspice, which contains pimento berries.

CLOVES The dry unopened flower bud of the tropical myrtle tree family. Cloves can be used whole or ground and impart a strong, warm spice to dishes.

COCONUT (BLOCK) Is made from coconut flesh and that has been dehydrated and compressed into a block shape. It needs to be chopped or shaved into your dish and adds the same flavour without the liquid.

COCONUT (FRUIT) This tropical fruit is used in many guises in Caribbean cooking – coconut milk in soups and stews, desiccated coconut to sweeten and in sweet dishes and coconut flesh in fresh dishes. Coconuts in the Caribbean are generally green – differing to the brown ones we normally think off – and these green specialities are known as 'Jelly coconuts'. This is due to their jelly like flesh inside.

COCONUT MILK (CANNED) A light milky liquid used in curries, stews and rice dishes. It has a high oil content and natural sugars, which commonly enhance flavours. Be mindful as dishes cooked with coconut milk are likely to go off the following day, even if refrigerated.

CONDENSED MILK Interchangeably known as carnation milk, is a thick and sweetened cows milk. Used traditionally for drinks or breakfasts. It is a staple cupboard item in the Caribbean islands.

CORNMEAL is the Caribbean term for polenta. This can be found from a coarse to fine texture and is not the same as cornflour/cornstarch. Cornmeal is the staple ingredient in making Jamaican Festivals (see page 140) and can sometimes be added to fried and boiled dumplings to provide a better texture.

CUMIN A dried spice that comes from the herbaceous plant, belonging to the same family as parsley and fennel. Traditionally, it is used more in other cultures but used in the Caribbean to enhance curries.

DUMPLINGS Jamaican dumplings are made from a mixture of flour, baking powder and salt and deep fried to make clouds of pure comfort food.

DUTCH OVEN Classic cast-iron cooking pot used to create stews and for anything that needs long slow cooking in the oven. It is called a Dutch pot in the Caribbean.

GARLIC POWDER A seasoning used to enhance garlic flavours and preferred due to its dissolvable qualities.

GINGER is a root with a fiery taste and aroma. Its skin is light brown with its flesh being a magnolia colour. Its used in a variety of dishes and drinks in the Caribbean to add heat and is known for its detoxing qualities. It can be smashed, grated, ground, dried or shredded – I prefer shredding to retain its texture.

GRENADINE A non-alcoholic syrup made from pomegranate and used to give cocktails a red colour.

HARD FOOD In Caribbean culture, earthy root vegetables, boiled in salted water with dumplings are commonly referred to as 'hard food'. This normally includes: yams, green banana, plantain, dumplings, sweetcorn, cabbage, chocho, cassava or pumpkin. It can be eaten on its own or served as a side to its dish.

ITAL FOOD One of the original forms of a 'plant-based diet'. However, Ital food tends to remain in its more natural state and doesn't attempt to recreate meat flavours or textures.

JACKFRUIT A tropical tree fruit that has quite a fibrous texture and is often bought canned and used as a meat substitute in dishes.

JAMAICAN DRIED SORREL (otherwise known as hibiscus flowers) A flower found on Caribbean islands, it's typically dried and turned into a festive drink with fruits and spices. When referring to sorrel it is commonly presumed to be the drink, not the spice.

JERK MARINADE A wet rub marinade used to preserve, flavour, smoke and season meats, fish and veg. Commonly found in the Caribbean islands and stems from the indigenous Awraks tribes and the smoke pits used use in the Caribbean to smoke and cook dishes. Jerk varies from different islands but generally infused, thyme, onions, garlic, pimentos and scallion. In modern years Jerk is readily available to buy and can additionally be found as dry rub.

JERK POWDER My own seasoning creation, inspired by South African influences such as peri-peri salt.

LIMES Smaller then a lemon, limes are small, round, green acidic fruits. They are commonly used in the Caribbean or Black British households to clean, and season meats and fish. They are generally preferred to lemons. Their skins are not waxed and some say they have a more intense flavour.

LYCHEE An Asian fruit similar to guinep (Spanish lime), that is eaten in the Caribbean. It's noticeable for its spikey shell and distinctive red colour. It can be eaten as a fruit or made into a juice.

MARIS PIPER A versatile potato, commonly found in the UK. I find it's great in all curries for its quick cooking speed and can be cooked skin on or off.

OAT MILK A plant-based substitute for dairy milk, made from oats. It can be easily swapped for another milk, but as I have become more conscious as a chef, this is my personal favourite.

PEAS A generic term used to describe either gungo peas, black-eyed peas or red kidney beans; the peas used in rice and peas – not to be confused with green peas. Peas are typically soaked overnight or used from a tin. If soaking overnight, the water is usually brined and discarded. Soaked peas have slightly more flavour than canned peas and are generally more cost effective.

PIMENTO BERRIES Also known as Jamaican pepper, these are the seeds from the pimento tree. They look like black peppercorns and can either be used whole or crushed as a flavouring in many dishes.

PLANTAIN A starchy fruit related to bananas, that can be eaten ripe or unripe and can be used in sweet or savoury dishes. Initially, plantains start off green and are savoury in taste when harvested, but mature into yellow plantain and become sweet in flavour when cooked. Green plantain is also referred to as green banana, but is not to be confused with the common fruit banana.

POT BOTTOM A Caribbean term for the caramelized (and still edible) bottom part of the dish, that has scorched on the base of a cooking pot. Often created from the sugars and starches found in ingredients and long cooking times. Pot bottom can be avoided by lining a pot with foil, particularly with rice or rice and peas.

RED LABEL APERITIF A brand of fortified wine that is particularly favoured in Jamaica. A good substitute is ruby port wine.

ROLLING BOIL This is the stage when entire contents of the pot is boiling at the highest possible temperature and remains at this heat without a drop in temperature. Generally vigorously bubbling and achieved with the lid on.

RUM A famously tropical alcohol made by fermenting and distilling sugarcane molasses to make a clear liquid, that is then usually aged in oak barrels. Used in many Caribbean drinks.

SALT FISH Also known as bacalao, it is simply salted and dried cod fish. Classily cooked as part of Jamaica's national dish, ackee and salt fish. It normally comes in a packet, and should be pinned and boned. For my recipes, I would advise using boneless saltfish. To use in cooking, the sailfish needs to be rehydrated by soaking in hot water several times to remove some of the salt.

SCOTCH BONNET PEPPERS The second hottest pepper in the world and my favourite chilli to use to add heat to my dishes.

SNAPPER A fish commonly found in the Caribbean sea and synonymous with Caribbean fish dishes. Known for its distinctive colourings (such as red snapper) and delicate texture. It is typically grilled, baked or fried and served with escovitch sauce (see page 67).

SOY SAUCE An Asian flavouring using in cooking as a flavour enhancer. I generally use it for this quality or as a substitute for browning.

SPRING ONION/SCALLION Part of the genus Allium family. I frequently split my spring onions, cooking with the white part and leaving the green part to add last, adding a better colour and vibrancy to my dish.

SWEET POTATO A sweet root plant identical to potatoes in texture and cooking methods. They are native to the South Americas but commonly found in British and Caribbean food. They can be two colours inside, white or orange, with the orange variety being sweeter.

THYME A fresh fragrant herb popular in Jamaican savoury dishes. I generally use fresh sprigs of thyme, snapped in half and added to dishes while I'm cooking to impart their flavour.

TURMERIC An Indian spice used to add colour to dishes, and commonly used in curries and stews.

VANILLA ESSENCE is most used in Caribbean baking and preferred over vanilla essence or the vanilla pod due to its ability to be easily diluted and lightness. Its commonly found in Caribbean-influenced markets or world food sections and has a noticeable brown colour.

VANILLA-FLAVOURED HIGH-PROTEIN DRINK A high-protein milk-based drink, generally used as a meal supplement. This is commonly found in punches and highly favoured due to is thick and creamy texture.

VEGETABLE BOUILLON POWDER This is a good-quality vegetable stock powder that I use in a lot of my cooking. I always use Marigold vegetable bouillon and would recommend its normal and vegan-friendly version.

YAMS A root vegetable that comes in different colours: white, purple and yellow and can be grown in the Caribbean or parts of Africa. Often added to stews, roasted or now even fried into chips/fries.

INDEX

PICTURE CREDITS

p.14 left, Laura/Adobe Stock 540057608; pp.14–15, PeskyMonkey/Adobe Stock 340230606; pp.34–35, Debbie Ann Powell/Adobe Stock 220997352; p.50 left, Peter/Adobe Stock 383518911; pp.50–51, Suchan/Adobe Stock 65328375; pp.70–71, Val Traveller/Adobe Stock326687138; pp.100–101, Karol Kozlowski/Adobe Stock 440768977; p.101 right, Debbie Ann Powell/Adobe Stock; p.118 left, Laura/Adobe Stock 540058408; pp.118–119, pirke/Adobe Stock 256443080; pp.144–145, LBSimms Photography/Adobe Stock 225891764; p.166 left, Enrico/Adobe Stock 313525516; pp.166–167, Frederico Rostagno/Adobe Stock 98503861.

ACKNOWLEDGEMENTS

Paradise Cove has such a long history that when thinking who to thank my mind is overwhelmed with the burgeoning amount of people who have all played a part in this story.

To my friends who I call family: Laura, Nancy and Gayle and Jean. You have all stood by me from the age of 17 and beyond and watched me conceive this idea right from the start. Remember when it was called Vieuxfort! You have seen me at my pitiful lows and soaring highs, but no matter what, never left my side. Paradise Cove wouldn't have half the recipes it does if you didn't endlessly taste my dishes, cakes and drinks. You're each a tool that strengthens a part of my life.

To some influential teachers: Mr Jones, Mrs Knowland, Mrs Harman and Dr Hoskins (to name a few). You enabled me to be myself and taught me to never give up. At various parts of my life, you instilled the ability of resilience. Whether it be primary school, secondary school or university, you provided sanctuary, shaping the man I am now. You enabled me to be a figure in my local community. I stand strong with the love and empathy you all gave me.

To the legends of Brixton: Some of my best hospitality years were spent under the guidance of the chefs Shelly, Kenneth, Miss India and Jannie. Through them I learned so much more than just the basics of Caribbean cooking. I learned about the culture I belong to. They were the strongest chefs I know and I strive to recreate their magic on a daily basis.

To Tina: You have been at my side since I was 11. You have watched me try and fail at every creative opportunity blessed to come my way. You helped me pick up paints and tools to open Paradise Cove, covered shifts when we had no staff, mentored my employees and just been an indescribable source of power that I give gratitude and thanks for. It takes a village to run Paradise Cove. You are my village.

To my publishers, RPS: Now you have utterly blown me away… and I am not easy to impress. I cannot begin to explain what this book means to me and what you have allowed me to demonstrate. Not only do I get to share my recipes with the world, you have enabled me to tell my story and that is priceless. I always said one day I would do it! Your entire team has worked incredibly hard and it is both my personal and professional joy to produce this piece of work with you. Together we are bringing Caribbean food to the many and that is really something special.

Lastly, myself: How could I not acknowledge myself? I worked every hour god sent to make my dream happen. I am creative, ambitious, cocky, wise but unwise, vulnerable and humble too. I never let a barrier stop me. I always knew I wanted a restaurant and by being my authentic self, I somehow made it happen at the age of 26. My recipes, my story, all the good, the bad and the ugly, brought me to this point and looking back, I just wouldn't change a single thing. I thank myself for being brave even when the odds were stacked against me… because for me, fear is temporary, but regret is permanent. And in every single Paradise Cove encounter that I have had, I do not possess one single regret.